ELECTRONICS IN PRACTICE

M P Horsey

Basil Blackwell

Acknowledgements

The author would like to thank John Blaker and
Andrew Hall for building and testing the circuits.

First published 1986

Published by Basil Blackwell Limited
108 Cowley Road
Oxford OX4 1JF

British Library Cataloguing in Publication Data

Horsey, M.P.
    Electronics in practice.
    1. Electronics
    I. Title
    537.5   TK7816
ISBN 0-631-90061-6

Typeset in 11/12½ American Typewriter
by Oxford Publishing Services, Oxford

Graphics by MicroInitiatives,
Knebworth, Herts.

Printed in Great Britain by
Butler and Tanner Ltd, Frome and London.

CONTENTS

HOW TO USE THIS BOOK

The book is divided into two parts. The first five chapters deal mainly with constructing circuits either on breadboard or stripboard. Chapter 1 is aimed at those who have never constructed an electronic circuit, and provides help with methods of construction, apparatus and components. Each circuit in the book has been tested, and is fully described, but you may need to refer to Chapter 6, to understand the 'How it works' sections.

Chapter 6 provides more details about the components used in the book. Other information is included to help you understand electronics and related subjects, such as the binary system.

Many readers will want to start building circuits as quickly as possible. They will not want to bother with too much theory at first. That is why much of the theory has been placed in Chapter 6. It will be needed if you want to learn more about the components and circuits, or wish to make alterations, or possibly find out why a circuit does not work.

If you are a beginner, start with the first or second project in Chapter 2. Then try at least one other project in Chapter 2 before advancing to projects in Chapters 3, 4 or 5. Always read the chapter introduction before starting to build a project in that chapter.

Electronics is a vital part of modern life. Whether you are studying it as a hobby or as part of a course, it will be of immense value to you in the future.

1 GETTING STARTED

Electrical Circuits

Throughout this book, we will use the convention that electricity flows from positive (+) to negative (−). In circuit diagrams it is often convenient to call the negative point **zero volts**. This helps especially when calculating the voltages throughout the circuit. Sometimes the zero volts line is connected to 'earth' (via a water pipe or copper rod driven into the earth outside). Another name often used is **ground**. You will frequently see the word 'ground' used even when the equipment is not connected to 'earth'. In this case it means a common point such as the metal case of the apparatus.

When electricity flows from positive to negative via a light bulb, we say that there is a complete circuit. The light bulb limits the flow of current round the circuit. If the light bulb is by-passed (as shown in Figure 1.1), electricity flows much more quickly and the battery quickly runs down. This is called a **short-circuit**. Clearly, short-circuits must always be avoided.

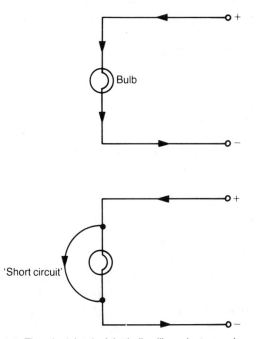

Figure 1.1 The wire 'shorting' the bulb will conduct a much greater current, which may damage other parts of the circuit or the battery etc.

Circuit diagrams

Figure 1.2 shows how wires are represented in circuit diagrams when they are connected with each other and when they are just crossing each other.

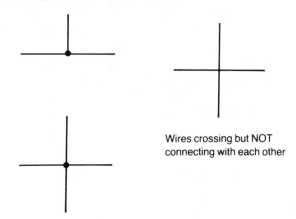

Wires connecting with each other

Figure 1.2

Switches

A switch will function at *any* of the places in Figure 1.3. The switch is a break in the

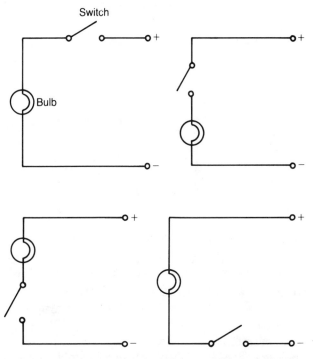

Figure 1.3 A switch may be placed in any of these positions to control the bulb

circuit which may be joined again by turning the switch on. When the circuit is broken, the flow of current stops. This happens regardless of which side of the bulb the break occurs.

Series and parallel circuits
As illustrated in Figure 1.4, bulbs (or any other components) may be wired in **series** by connecting them in a 'chain' one after another. It is important to note that if any component breaks down, the circuit is broken and the flow of current will stop through *all* the series components.

Bulbs (or other components) which are wired in **parallel** are connected across each other. If one breaks down, the others will continue to work.

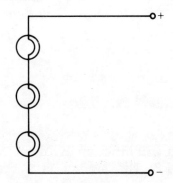

3 bulbs wired in series

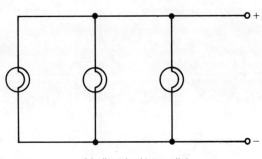

3 bulbs wired in parallel

Figure 1.4

Direct current and alternating current
Direct current (d.c.) is the type which flows from a battery. It flows in *one direction* through a circuit. Most electronic circuits require d.c. They will burn out if supplied with a.c.

Alternating current (a.c.) continuously changes direction. In other words the terminals of an a.c. power unit alternately change from positive to negative and back again. A battery cannot supply a.c. This type of current is often supplied by a generator. Power stations generate a.c. In fact our 240 V mains supply alternates at a frequency of 50 hertz. (Hertz (Hz) means 'cycles per second', where a 'cycle' is a complete change from positive to negative and back to positive.) Power units which convert our mains supply to a low voltage normally change the alternating current into direct current as well. The method used is described in Chapter 3.

Equipment You Will Need

You may be surprised by how little equipment is needed to begin this absorbing subject. First decide if you wish to build the circuits on **breadboard** (prototype board) or **stripboard**. Breadboard is for temporary circuits which may be taken apart and the components re-used. You will *not* require a soldering iron. Stripboard is for permanent circuits and you will need to solder the components in place. However, do not be put off by the thought of soldering. It is a simple and very reliable method of joining wires and components. Nearly all the circuits in this book include layout diagrams for both types of construction.

Essential items for breadboard construction are:

- breadboard (e.g. Verobloc as illustrated in this book)
- small plastic-handled electrical screwdriver
- pair of wire-strippers/cutters (Don't use scissors or your teeth. You will damage them!)
- reel of red, pvc coated, single strand (i.e. solid core) copper wire, about 23 SWG†
- reel of black pvc wire as above.
- components as listed for each project

Bare copper wire (about 24 SWG) is useful for very short links, but invites problems from short-circuits. Multistrand wire is difficult to push into the holes in the board.

† Note: SWG stands for 'standard wire gauge' and *increases* as the thickness of the wire *decreases*.

Additional items for stripboard constructions are:

- stripboard (e.g. Veroboard)
- small soldering iron (e.g. general purpose 17 W type)
- multicore solder
- stripboard track cutter or small drill
- hacksaw for cutting stripboard

Other items that you may find helpful are:

- bare multi-strand wire for soaking up and removing unwanted solder, or a solder sucker
- drill and drill bits for preparing cases in which to house your circuits
- pair of tweezers — particularly helpful with breadboard construction
- soldering iron stand
- voltmeter, reading to about 10 V or a multimeter measuring voltage, current and resistance, to trace faults in circuits.

Ordering Parts

Unless you live near a good electronics supplies shop, components will need to be ordered by post. This is much simpler than it sounds, since most mail order firms are very efficient and maintain a fast and reliable service. Any electronics magazine will contain advertisements by major suppliers, and bargains may often be found. Most firms supply order forms (although orders may be made without these, simply by quoting the stock numbers) and accept payment by cheque, postal order or credit card (e.g. for telephone orders).

It would be impossible to list all the firms which provide a good service, but you could do little better than start with the catalogue from Maplin Electronic Supplies. Apart from endless pages of components, the catalogue contains a great deal of useful information.

Another firm worth mentioning is R.S. Components. Again, a very comprehensive catalogue is produced, but parts are not available to the 'general public'. Instead, orders must be placed through a retailer, school, or college. R.S. Components offer a

very fast service; goods are normally despatched the same day an order is received.

A word of caution. Some 'High Street' shops stock electronics components, but their prices may be much higher than specialist suppliers. Always compare prices before buying.

Methods of Construction

Constructing on breadboard

The type of breadboard illustrated in this book is Verobloc, although other types of breadboard may also be used. It is designed for circuits which employ a variety of components including integrated circuits (ICs). Look carefully at Figure 1.5 which shows how the lines of sockets are internally connected by metal strips.

Components may be used many times over, to make different circuits. Various accessories are available which slot into the breadboard, enabling potentiometers (e.g. volume controls) and switches to be mounted and connected.

This type of system is ideal for trying out prototype (newly designed) circuits. It also enables the beginner to build many circuits quickly and cheaply.

Wires and leads should normally be placed in the sockets indicated in the diagrams. Sometimes this will not be possible, but if you use another socket, *ensure that it is connected by the same metal strip.* Pushing a wire or lead into a different row of contacts will prevent the circuit working.

Wires and component leads must be straight and clean. Cut off dirty or kinked ends. You will find that solid wires are easier to fit than stranded wires. Where stranded wires cannot be avoided, they must be very firmly twisted together. When using insulated wires strip off about 1 cm of insulation. Ensure that the wire is pushed right into the socket — it must connect with the metal strip inside the breadboard.

Components may be fitted in the same way, and the leads from the component will need to be bent into position. Avoid bending

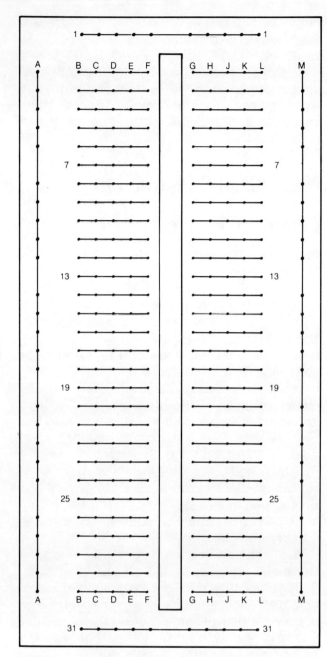

Figure 1.5 Diagram showing how the breadboard sockets are interconnected

the leads too near the body of the component — they tend to break off. This applies especially to transistors and similar components. The circuit arrangements in this book are designed to avoid this problem.

When the circuit is finished, check carefully to ensure that bare wires are not touching one another. Check that transistors, diodes, integrated circuits and elec-

trolytic capacitors are fitted the correct way round. Connect the power supply or battery the correct way round. The 5 V regulator described in Chapter 3 will power nearly all the circuits in this book and has a limited current output. This will protect your components, even if your circuit is wired incorrectly.

Constructing on stripboard

Stripboard (often sold as Veroboard) consists of a thin sheet punched with holes on a 0.1 inch (or 0.15 inch) matrix (i.e. it has a pattern of holes spread at 0.1 inch intervals). The board may be plain, or have copper strips or 'tracks' on one side. The copper strip (known as copper-clad) board with a 0.1 inch matrix is the one used in this book.

Always buy the size required, or larger. Very large boards may be sawn to the required size. In some circuits the copper tracks have to be cut or broken. This may be achieved with the aid of a drill, or more simply with a special tool made for the purpose; a 'spot face cutter' or track cutter.

Place the stripboard with the *copper tracks underneath*, and running *left to right*. A common mishap with beginners is to place the stripboard so that the tracks run up and down. A circuit constructed in this way will be totally wrong.

A fine fibre-tip pen is of immense value in marking the tracks A, B, C etc., as indicated on the layout diagram. This reduces the chance of mistakes, particularly in complicated circuits. All markings should be on the non copper side (i.e. the component side).

If breaks are required in the copper tracks, mark the positions of these on both sides of the board. Then use a track cutter (or spot face cutter) or small drill to break the track completely, leaving no traces of copper to cause a short circuit.

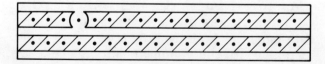

Figure 1.6 Stripboard, copper side up. The break in the track is made with a spot face cutter or small drill.

A break made in the wrong place may have to be re-joined. Avoid the temptation to use a large blob of solder — it will probably join tracks together, but not the ones required! Thread a short piece of bare wire through the hole on either side of the break and solder it in place to make the track complete again.

Each component or wire link should be placed on the non copper side of the board. Its lead should be pushed through the correct holes as shown in the construction diagram. If you have to use a different hole (for example, because a component is larger than illustrated), ensure that the hole you choose is connected to the same copper track. This normally means that you may move components *sideways* (with the tracks running *left to right*) — but check that you have not gone past a break in the track.

Many circuits require the use of wire links to electrically join copper tracks. As mentioned earlier, any type of copper wire may be used, but thin, tinned copper wire is ideal. This is bare copper wire, which is silvery in appearance. When fitting wire links, *do not* cut them to size; take a long piece of wire, solder in one end, then pull the other end through the appropriate hole before cutting it off. You will be surprised at how quickly and easily wire links can be fitted in this way.

The order in which components are fitted is of little importance, although more delicate components, such as transistors, should be left until last. It is normally more convenient to begin with the smallest parts (e.g. wire links, resistors) although some constructors prefer to start at one end of the board, and work across.

Check that diodes, transistors, thyristors and electrolytic capacitors are the correct way round. If possible, the body of the component should lie flat against the board. However, this does not apply to some capacitors. Transistors and thyristors are best mounted with their bodies well above the board, and dual-in-line (DIL) integrated circuits should be housed in DIL sockets.

Take care not to touch the body of the component with the soldering iron. There should be little risk of this, as the components are on the non copper side of the stripboard. All soldering is done on the copper side.

Most circuits require wires linking the stripboard to other items, such as a battery. Use insulated wires for this purpose, not forgetting to strip off about 0.5 cm of insulation before connecting. These wires are best fitted last, to avoid a tangled mess!

To summarise:
1 Place the stripboard with copper tracks underneath, and running left to right (not up and down).
2 Mark some of the tracks and holes on the non copper side, with a fibre-tip pen.
3 If necessary, break the copper tracks where indicated.
4 Fit and solder the wire links and components, as indicated in the constructional layout diagram, starting with the smallest.
5 Solder in additional wires as required.

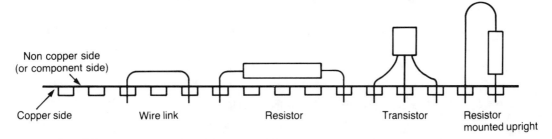

Figure 1.7 Mounting components on stripboard

Other Methods of Construction

Printed circuit board

Printed circuit board, known as p.c.b., is the most advanced method of construction and is similar to stripboard, except that the copper tracks are arranged in a special pattern designed for the circuit being constructed. Thus a printed circuit board must be designed to suit the project, before building can begin.

It is sometimes possible to purchase a ready-made p.c.b. for a particular project. If such a p.c.b. is not available, this method of construction cannot be recommended for the beginner.

Tag strip

Tag strips offer a very simple method of construction, particularly where only a few components are required. The 5 V regulator in Chapter 3 is built on a tag strip. Drawing pins pushed into soft wood can serve a similar purpose, although a great deal of heat is required to make a successful solder joint on a drawing pin and this could damage sensitive components.

How to Solder

Before use, it is essential to clean the soldering iron 'bit', at the end of the soldering iron. It is best cleaned when hot, and may be firmly wiped across a damp sponge or rough paper. Note that iron clad bits should not be filed.

After cleaning, and especially if new, the bit should be 'tinned' with solder. This involves touching the hot soldering iron bit against multicore solder (solder containing cores of flux), until the bit is completely coated. Then wipe it against a damp sponge or rough paper to remove any surplus solder. The bit is now tinned, and ready for use.

When soldering, all surfaces should be clean and dry. This applies especially to copper tracks, which soon attract dirt. Various materials and chemicals are sold to clean copper boards or, alternatively, abrasive paper may be used.

Aim to use the minimum amount of heat necessary to achieve a good joint. Too much heat may cause damage. However, too little heat will result in a 'dry joint' — that is, a joint which appears secure but will not conduct electricity. Dry joints account for many failed projects!

Place the soldering iron bit firmly against the copper track *and* wire being soldered. Apply the solder quite quickly at the point where the bit is touching the copper track. It will flow onto the track, and form a 'blob' around the wire being soldered. Remove the soldering iron. As the solder cools, it should form a shiny blob, firmly bonded to the copper track. (See Figure 1.8.) If it appears very dull, and has not flowed into place against the copper, it is probably a dry joint (i.e. too little heat has been used). In this case, simply apply the iron again, with a little more solder.

It is unlikely that any solder will flow across to another track, unless far too much is used. If solder has to be removed, flexible multi-stranded wire will 'soak up' hot solder. Desolder braid is available for the same purpose, or a proper solder sucker may be purchased, which makes light work of solder removal and de-soldering.

Never use the soldering iron as a 'spoon' to carry solder, and never try to prod the solder into place. (This almost guarantees a 'dry joint'.) Simply keep the soldering iron firmly against the parts being soldered, and push the solder onto the tip of the bit. As the

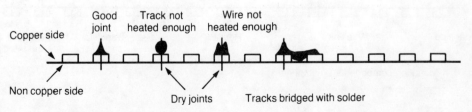

Figure 1.8 Soldering on stripboard

temperature rises, the solder will flow into place – *without* any poking or pushing!

Flexible wire connections should be tinned before pushing the bare wire through the holes. This involves coating the wire with solder – a task which takes very little time and ensures a good bond without the risk of odd strands of wire bridging the tracks.

When soldering is complete, the leads may be trimmed by cutting the surplus wire·close to the solder joints. Always inspect each joint carefully, being especially watchful for dry joints and small bridges of solder joining one track with another. Run a screwdriver blade between each pair of tracks to clean out odd spots of solder. Never forget the importance of a neat layout, and clean, well made joints. Given this, the circuit stands a good chance of working the first time.

De-soldering

Hopefully, you will not need to read this section! Solder may be removed by any of the methods described above. Unfortunately, components are sometimes damaged during this operation and very cheap items, such as resistors, are probably best discarded unless great care is taken. If a transistor has been mounted as outlined earlier (with its body well above the stripboard), it may be possible to cut its leads just above the non copper side of the board. If a transistor must be de-soldered, use as little heat as possible, and wait a few moments after removing the solder from one joint before tackling the next. This will allow the heat to dissipate.

Special 'heat shunts', or 'heat sink tweezers' are available, which clip to the leads of heat sensitive components, such as transistors. Pliers can also be used for this.

Selecting Your Components

Components lists are provided for each project, and more details about the components are given in Chapter 6. This section provides a short general guide to help you get started very quickly.

Transistors: Throughout this book the BC184L is specified. This is an inexpensive, general purpose npn transistor. In most cases the BC182L and BC183L will work just as well. Note that the 'L' is important. The BC184 transistor (without the 'L') has leads in a different order. The BC108C transistor may also be used, but again its leads are arranged differently – see Figure 1.9.

Figure 1.9 Transistors

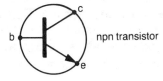

npn transistor

Types BC184L, BC183L, BC182L — as used throughout this book

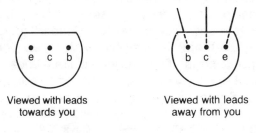

Viewed with leads towards you   Viewed with leads away from you

Types BC184, BC183, BC182

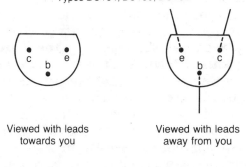

Viewed with leads towards you   Viewed with leads away from you

Types BC108, BC108B, BC108C (BC107, BC109)

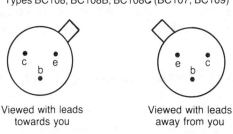

Viewed with leads towards you   Viewed with leads away from you

Diodes: The types specified are either 1N4001 or 1N4148. You may use the 1N4001 type throughout if you wish, but a 1N4148 type must not be used where a 1N4001 is specified.

Resistors: Where 'any type' is specified, it is best to buy the cheapest — and normally the smallest. The components lists give the value, in ohms, of each resistor required, and its colours. In some cases the value is not critical and another may be tried, *but* — you could cause damage by using a *lower* value in some instances. If in doubt use the value given. Watch out for the letters 'k' and 'M' in the resistor values. 'k' means times a thousand, 'M' means times a million. (Full details are in Chapter 6.) Where 'presets' are specified, again select the cheapest, miniature (described as 'sub-miniature' by some suppliers), horizontal mounting types.

Capacitors: Where 'any type' is specified, in general, buy the cheapest. Some small-value capacitors are specially designed for printed circuit boards and have short leads. This can be a problem, especially with breadboard constructions. The values in this book are quoted in microfarads (μF), or picofarads (pF). Some suppliers list values in nanofarads (nF). Note that 0.01 μF=10 nF; 0.022 μF=22 nF; 0.1 μF=100 nF. Full details of these units are given in Chapter 6.

When buying larger value capacitors (above 1 μF), an electrolytic type will normally be chosen. In general, a **single ended** type (with both wires at the same end) is the most convenient but **axial lead** types (wires at opposite ends) may also be used. If you wish to stand this type vertically, one lead can be bent round the capacitor. (See the vertically mounted resistor in Figure 1.7). Electrolytic capacitors tend to have a lower working voltage than other capacitors. Do check that the capacitor's working voltage is greater than the low-voltage supply you are using.

Light emitting diodes (LEDs): In all these circuits a general purpose red LED, designed for about 10 mA current, is best. Other colours may be used, but they may appear less bright.

Solid state buzzer: Buy a 6 V type. Avoid old fashioned types with make-and-break contacts. These produce a high voltage

which can damage your circuit unless a protective diode is fitted. You will see how such a diode is fitted in any of the circuits using a relay, as this also produces a high voltage. Any **solid state** (sometimes called 'transistorised') buzzer, bleeper or siren will not require a protective diode.

Relay: Check that the coil voltage is correct, bearing in mind that the actual voltage across the relay coil will be about 0.5 V less than your supply. The resistance of the coil should be at least 100 Ω (6 V type) or 150 Ω (12 V type). Check that the contacts are rated to carry the voltage and current you wish to switch on and off. Reed relays are particularly useful as they have a higher coil resistance and wider voltage range — but their contacts have a lower rating. Relays produce a high voltage when switching off (known as 'back e.m.f.'). The circuits in this book include a diode in parallel with the relay coil to short-circuit this high voltage spike and protect your circuit. Do not leave out this diode — even though the circuit will appear to work without it. Also, ensure that you fit it the correct way round as illustrated in each layout.

Integrated circuits: Most of the ICs in this book are 'dual-in-line' (DIL) types with pins down each side. Buy the type number specified. When using stripboard with this type, also buy a DIL IC socket with the correct number of pins. If the IC is a CMOS type, do not unpack it until you have read the special instructions in Chapter 4. When checking the codes stamped on the IC, ignore the various numbers and letters printed in addition to the code itself. It is important to fit the IC the correct way round, with pin 1 at the corner indicated in the layout diagrams. Figure 1.10 shows how a notch or small (off centre) dot is placed near pin 1. Note also the pin numbering system used.

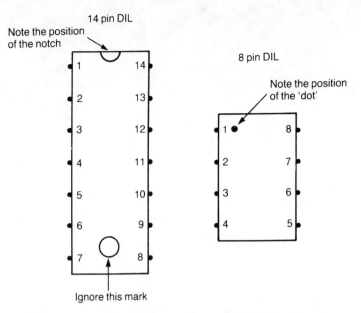

Figure 1.10 Arrangements of pins in 'dual-in-line' (DIL) integrated circuits
(Note: 16 pin ICs are also used in this book. Both the 'notch' and/or the 'dot' (nearest pin 1) may be found on any of the ICs used, regardless of the number of pins.)

Power Supplies

The voltage required for each project is stated in each chapter and/or project introduction, but to summarise, all the projects in Chapters 2 and 3 may be powered from a 9 V d.c. supply. A PP3 battery is very convenient, and PP3 battery clips are available to connect to your circuit. Most of these projects will also work on a 5 V d.c. supply, and the 5 V regulator described in Chapter 3 is ideal since the current it will supply is limited — thus protecting your circuit if it is wired incorrectly. The 5 V regulator is particularly useful for classroom work, and a set may be constructed even by inexperienced pupils.

The projects in Chapter 4 require a 5 V d.c. supply (or 4.5 V battery). A 9 V supply will destroy the integrated circuits used in Chapter 4. The 5 V regulator is again ideal.

The computer projects in Chapter 5 will normally use the computer's own 5 V supply.

2 CONSTRUCTING SIMPLE PROJECTS

This chapter contains constructional details for the following projects:

1 Soil moisture indicator
2 Water sensing bleeper
3 Steady hand tester
4 Light activated switch
5 Sound to light unit
6 Intruder alarm

Each circuit may be built on breadboard or stripboard, and full layout diagrams are included for both. They all perform a useful function and illustrate important concepts in electronics.

Finished stripboard circuits may be mounted in cases, and a wide range of plastic and metal cases is available. When using metal cases, ensure that the metal parts of stripboard etc. are not allowed to touch the metal case, as a 'short-circuit' may occur. Each circuit may be operated from a small PP3, 9 V battery or a 5 V d.c. supply.

Components lists

1 Where a LED is used, an alternative series resistor is indicated for operation on 5 V. This is to obtain the maximum LED brightness.
2 Where a relay is used, the circuit may be operated on any voltage from 5 to 12 V — to suit the relay you buy.
3 The fourth resistor band is denoted by the word 'any'. This means that the fourth band, if present, may be silver, gold, red or brown. (See Chapter 6 for details if necessary.)
4 If constructing on breadboard, some parts are not required. This is indicated by '(not BB)' in the components lists.

Soil Moisture Indicator

Suitable supply voltage: 5 to 12 V d.c.

Applications

Testing moisture in soil; transistor tester.

This device has two probes which are placed in the soil being tested. If the soil is dry, nothing happens. If the soil is damp, the LED lights up.

Components

Semiconductors
Tr1   transistor BC184L
L1   light emitting diode (LED), about 10 mA; red, any size

Resistors (any type)
R1   1 kΩ (brown, black, red, 'any')
R2   1 kΩ
      or 270 Ω (red, violet, brown, 'any') for 5 V operation

Miscellaneous
stripboard, at least 10 holes by 6 tracks (not BB)
battery clip for PP3 battery

How it works

Very little electricity will flow through dry soil. If the soil is damp, a small electric current will flow. This is insufficient to light up a bulb, or even a LED.

In this circuit (Figure 2.1), the transistor is used as a switch. The small current which flows through damp soil is fed into the transistor base (b). Resistor R1 prevents too much current flowing to the base, especially if the probes are accidentally touched together. The flow of current to the base of Tr1 switches it on, and a much larger current flows from the collector (c) to the emitter (e). This flow of current causes the LED to light, with resistor R2 limiting the flow to a reasonable level.

Breadboard construction (Figure 2.2)

See Chapter 1 for general notes on breadboard construction.
1 Cut one piece of bare wire to make a short wire link, and insert as shown in Figure 2.2.
2 Fit the two resistors.
3 Fit the transistor and LED the *correct way round*.
4 Fit the two bare wires for the 'probes'.
5 Fit the two insulated wires for the positive (+, red) and negative (−, black) supplies.

Stripboard construction (Figure 2.3)

See Chapter 1 for general notes on stripboard construction. Using Figure 2.3 as a guide:
1 Label the stripboard, A, B, etc., on the *opposite* side to the copper tracks, ensuring that the tracks run *left to right*. Remember to place all components on the non copper side.

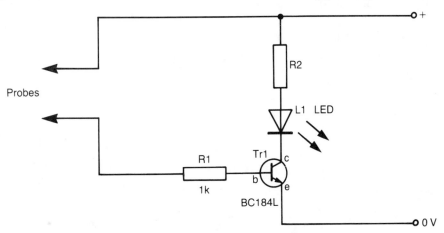

Figure 2.1 Soil moisture indicator: circuit diagram

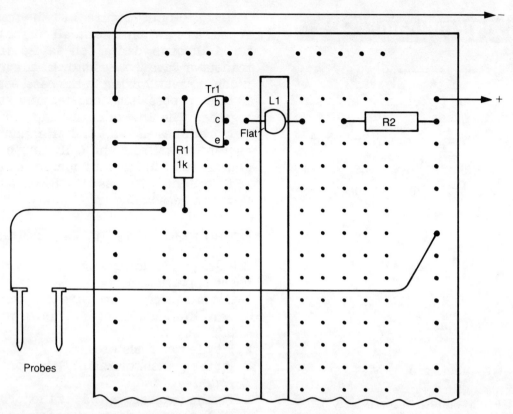

Figure 2.2 Soil moisture indicator: layout diagram for breadboard construction

2 Solder in resistors R1 and R2.

3 Solder in the transistor, ensuring that it is exactly the same way round as shown in the diagram (looking from above, with the wires pointing downwards). Do not push the transistor body too near the stripboard.

4 The LED may be soldered directly to the stripboard, or it may be connected with wires. Whichever method you prefer, ensure that it is connected the same way round, as shown in the diagram.

5 Connect the other wires to the stripboard, and connect the PP3 battery clip —

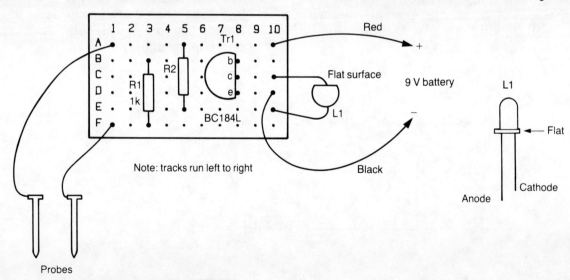

Figure 2.3 Soil moisture indicator: layout diagram for stripboard construction

remembering that red is positive, black is negative.

6 The probes may be made from any conducting materials; for example, two nails, or even the ends of two stiff wires.

7 The stripboard and battery may be housed in a small plastic case, or an old tobacco tin. In the latter case, ensure that the copper tracks cannot short-circuit through the metal of the case (e.g. line the case with insulating tape or cardboard).

8 Carefully check the circuit board for mistakes, and check for tracks which have been accidentally bridged with solder.

Testing

Read the section on 'Fault finding' in Chapter 6.

1 Connect a suitable battery or power supply *the correct way round*.

2 The LED should not light up when the probes are not touching each other. If it does, then disconnect the supply and check for mistakes.

3 If all is well, touch the probes together. The LED should now light up. If it does not, then disconnect the supply and check for mistakes.

4 Finally, hold the probes a few centimetres apart and place them in some water. The LED should light up. You will find that it will also light up if the probes are placed in damp soil, but not if placed in very dry soil.

Transistor tester

This circuit may be used as a simple transistor tester. The probe connections should be joined to a switch. If this switch turns the LED on *and* off, the transistor (Tr1) must be working. If the LED will not light, the transistor is faulty; if the LED remains on even with the switch off, the transistor has a short-circuit and is equally useless.

On breadboard you can simply 'plug in' the transistor you wish to test. On stripboard you could purchase a transistor holder. This will also enable you to plug in transistors for testing. This simple device will test BC184L, BC183L and BC182L transistors. To test other small npn types, check the positions of the base, collector and emitter connections carefully (see Chapter 1).

Water Sensing Bleeper

Suitable supply voltage: 5 to 9 V d.c.

Applications

Warning of rain on washing day, washing machine leak detector, blind person's cup level indicator, bath level warning, etc.

This is a similar project to the soil moisture indicator, but signals the presence of water by means of a solid state buzzer or bleeper. It uses very little current, unless actually bleeping, and may be left switched on for long periods without running down the battery.

Components

Semiconductors
Tr1 transistor BC184L

Resistors (any type)
R1 1 kΩ (brown, black, red, 'any')

Miscellaneous
B1 buzzer, solid state (6 V)
stripboard, at least 10 holes by 5 tracks (not BB)
stripboard for sensing pad (about 10 holes by 4 tracks) (not BB)
PP3 battery clip
long connecting wires between main circuit and sensing pad

How it works

The circuit diagram is shown in Figure 2.4. When the sensing pad is dry no current flows between its tracks, and thus no current is able to flow into the base of the transistor. The transistor therefore remains switched off. When the sensing pad is made damp, a very small current of electricity flows from one track to the next, and then to the base of Tr1, via resistor R1. This resistor protects the transistor against excessive current. Current into the base of Tr1 switches it on, and a much larger current is able to flow through the buzzer, making it sound.

Breadboard construction (Figure 2.5)

1 Fit the short wire link as shown.
2 Fit the resistor.
3 Fit the transistor the correct way round, with the flat edge towards the centre.
4 Connect the solid state buzzer the correct way round.
5 Connect the water detector which, again, may be simply two pieces of bare wire as shown, or two nails.
6 Connect the positive (+, red) and negative (−, black) supplies.

Stripboard construction (Figure 2.6)

1 Label the stripboard, A, B, etc., on the *opposite* side to the copper tracks, ensuring that the tracks run *left to right*.
2 Solder in the resistor R1.
3 Solder in the transistor, ensuring that it is *exactly the same way round* as shown in the diagram (looking from above, with the wires pointing downwards). Do not push the transistor body too near the stripboard.

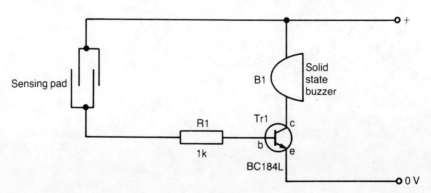

Figure 2.4 Water sensing bleeper: circuit diagram

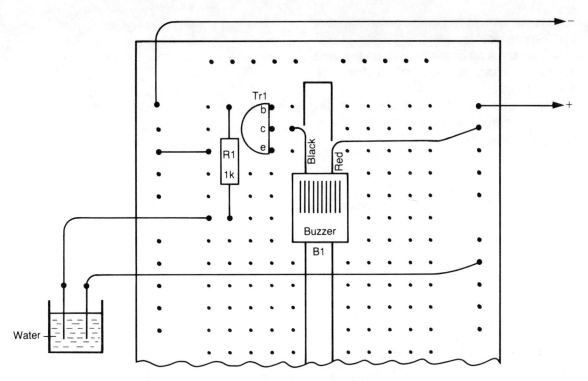

Figure 2.5 Water sensing bleeper: layout diagram for breadboard construction

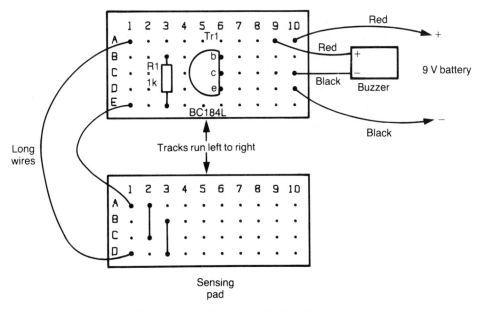

Figure 2.6 Water sensing bleeper: layout diagram for stripboard construction

4 Solder the buzzer connections to the strip-board, ensuring that the colours are correct. (Red is positive (+); black is negative (−).)

5 Connect the other wires to the stripboard, and connect the PP3 battery clip the *correct way round*.

6 Solder the wires to the sensing pad and join the tracks with wire links, as shown in the diagram. When connecting wire links, it is best to thread the wire through the first hole, solder, pass into the next hole as indicated, and solder — before cutting to length. This is much easier

than cutting the wire links to the correct length before soldering.

7 The stripboard and battery may be housed in a small case, as described for the previous project.

8 Carefully check the circuit board for mistakes, and ensure that no tracks have been accidentally bridged with solder.

9 When the circuit is put to use, it may be necessary to connect long wires between the sensing pad and the circuit. Any wire may be used for this, such as ordinary twin flex.

Testing

Read the section on 'fault finding' in Chapter 6.

1 Connect a suitable battery or power supply *the correct way round*.

2 The buzzer should not sound. If it does, switch off and check for mistakes — especially bridged tracks, or the transistor, buzzer or PP3 clip connected the wrong way round.

3 Wet your finger and place it on the copper tracks of the sensing pad. The buzzer should sound. When you remove your finger, moisture left on the pad may continue to cause the buzzer to sound. Eventually, the moisture should dry up, and the buzzer will stop sounding.

Steady Hand Tester

Suitable supply voltage: 5 to 9 V d.c.

Applications

This type of circuit may be used for any warning system where you want the sound to continue until switched off.

Popular in fetes throughout the country, the steady hand tester consists of a wire loop which must be moved from one end of a stiff wire to the other. If the loop touches the stiff wire, a circuit is completed and a buzzer or bell sounds.

If the loop touches the stiff wire for a very short time, the bell or buzzer may produce a very short sound, making it difficult to tell whether the loop really did touch the wire. The circuit described overcomes this problem by making the buzzer continue to sound *after* the loop has touched the stiff wire. The buzzer can only be silenced by switching off the 'master switch'. The user is therefore prevented from cheating.

Components

Semiconductors
Th1 thyristor type C106
   (Note: there may be another letter after this code, e.g. C106D. This letter is not important in this circuit).

Resistors (any type)
R1 1 kΩ (brown, black, red, 'any')
R2 1 kΩ
R3 1 kΩ

Miscellaneous
S1 on/off switch (any type)
B1 buzzer (solid state, 6 V)
stripboard, at least 13 holes by 5 tracks (not BB)
battery clip for PP3 battery
base and supports as indicated in Figure 2.9
thick wire to fix to supports
thick wire for wire loop
wire loop holder (an old pen may be used)

How it works

A thyristor (silicon controlled rectifier, or SCR) behaves rather like a transistor, in that a small flow of current into its **gate** (G) causes a larger flow from **anode** (A) to **cathode** (C). However, unlike a transistor the thyristor remains switched on even if the flow of current to the gate stops. It will continue to conduct until the supply of current via the anode is switched off.

The circuit diagram is shown in Figure 2.7. When switch S1 is closed (switched on), no current can flow through the buzzer, as the thyristor Th1 is 'non conducting' (switched off). Resistor R2 holds the thyristor gate at zero volts, ensuring that it is not triggered accidentally – especially by electrical noise in your body if you happen to touch the wire loop.

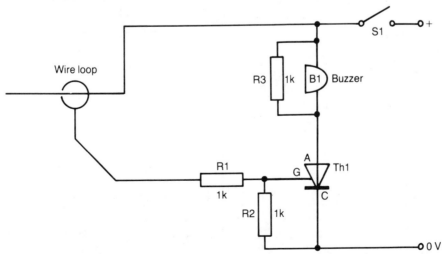

Figure 2.7 Steady hand tester: circuit diagram

If the wire loop touches the stiff wire, a small current flows through resistor R1 to the gate of the thyristor. (The purpose of R1 is to limit this flow of current to a safe level, to protect the thyristor). The current causes the thyristor to conduct (switch on), and current now flows from its anode to cathode, thus activating the buzzer. The buzzer can be silenced only by switching off the circuit.

The buzzer may allow the current to flow in pulses rather than continuously, causing the thyristor to switch off. Thus resistor R3 is included to provide a path for the current, ensuring that the thyristor remains on.

Note the importance of switch S1. Some constructors may be tempted to omit this switch, especially if the circuit is driven from a power unit with a switch built in. However, an electric charge may be left on the power unit's smoothing capacitor for some time after it is turned off. Although this charge will eventually reduce to zero, it may prevent the thyristor switching off for an appreciable time.

Breadboard construction (Figure 2.8)

1 Fit the wire link and resistors.
2 Fit the thyristor vertically, noting that the metal tab is towards the right with the plastic body towards the left.
3 Fit the buzzer the correct way round and other wires as shown, noting that red is positive (+).

Stripboard construction (Figure 2.9)

1 Label the stripboard.
2 Solder in the resistors R1, R2 and R3.
3 Solder in the thyristor, ensuring that it is connected the correct way round.
4 Solder all the connecting leads to the stripboard. Fairly long wires may be needed to join the stripboard to the wire loop etc.

The wire loop may be made from a 20 cm length of thick, bare wire. Bend one end into a loop of about 2 to 3 cm diameter, and pass

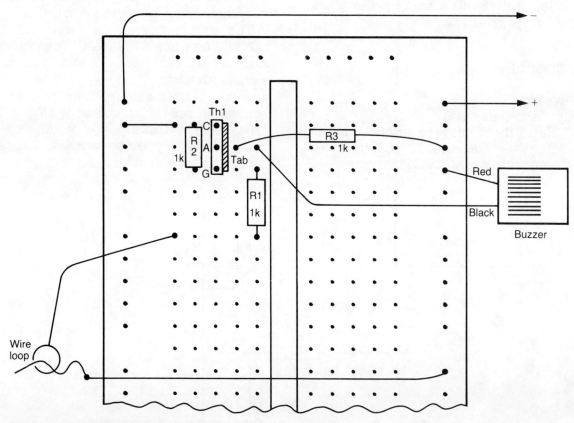

Figure 2.8 Steady hand tester: layout diagram for breadboard construction
(Note: There is 1 wire link.)

the straight end through the case of an old ballpoint pen as shown in Figure 2.9. A more flexible insulated wire may be employed to connect the thick wire to the stripboard.

The ends of the bare stiff wire should be mounted on two supports, possibly made from wood and mounted on a wooden base. A small piece of insulation (insulation tape may be used), should be placed at each end of the stiff wire to enable the wire loop to hang without setting off the buzzer.

Testing

Read the section on 'Fault finding' in Chapter 6.

1 Connect a suitable battery *the correct way round*.
2 Switch on S1. The buzzer should not sound. If it does, switch off and check for mistakes, especially bridged tracks, or the thyristor connected incorrectly.
3 Touch the wire loop against the bare stiff wire. The buzzer should now sound. Separate the wire loop and stiff wire. The buzzer should continue to sound, until S1 is switched off.
4 Switch on S1 again. The buzzer should not sound until the wire loop makes contact with the stiff wire again.

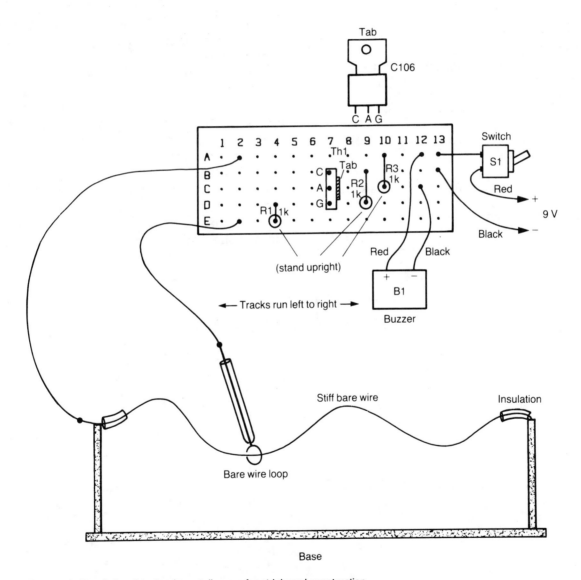

Figure 2.9 Steady hand tester: layout diagram for stripboard construction

Light Activated Switch

Suitable supply voltage: 5 to 12 V d.c.

Applications

Automatic light, car parking light, burglar (light beam) sensor, automatic curtain operator, etc.

Components

Semiconductors
Tr1   transistor BC184L
L1   LED, about 10 mA; red, any size
D1   diode 1N4148 or 1N4001 (required only if relay is used)

Resistors (any type)
LDR CdS cell, type ORP12
R1   150 Ω (brown, green, brown, 'any')
R2   1 kΩ (brown, black, red, 'any')
R3   1 kΩ
       or 270 Ω (red, violet, brown, 'any') for operation on 5 V
VR1 preset, min. horizontal, 47 kΩ.

Miscellaneous
stripboard, at least 20 holes by 8 tracks (not BB)
battery clip for PP3 battery
relay (if required)

How it works

Several light sensing devices are available, and the one chosen for this project is a **light dependent resistor (LDR)**, type ORP12. This type of resistor is also known as a cadmium sulphide cell (CdS cell). In darkness, its resistance is about 10 million ohms. This falls to about 100 ohms in bright sunlight.

Projects 1 and 2 used an 'all or nothing' approach. No adjustment was provided for the user and the circuits did not distinguish between 'slightly moist', 'very moist' etc. A circuit which reacts to light must include some adjustment, as each person may want it to react to a different level of light. Thus the circuit is a little more complicated and includes a variable resistor (preset) to allow user control.

The circuit is shown in Figure 2.10. Resistor R1 is connected in series with variable resistor VR1, so that the total resistance cannot be below 150 Ω, even if VR1 is set to zero. This protects the LDR from excessive current. Consider VR1 and R1 as a single resistor, connected in series to the LDR. The supply will be divided between this 'single resistor' and the LDR; for example, if they are of equal resistance, the voltage (potential) at the point where they join will be half

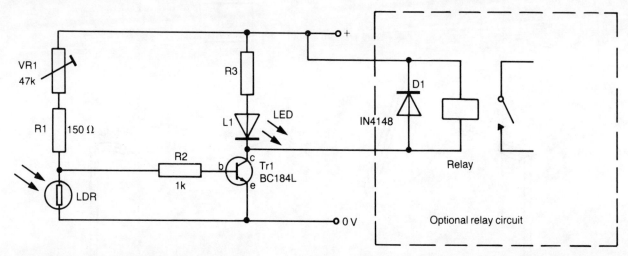

Figure 2.10 Light activated switch: circuit diagram

the supply. If the LDR's resistance decreases, this voltage will fall.

The BC184L transistor will not switch on until the voltage at its base rises to about 0.6 V. Thus if the resistance of the LDR is low compared with VR1 and R1, less than 0.6 V will be available at the transistor base, and the transistor will not switch on. If the light level on the LDR falls, its resistance will increase and the voltage at the transistor base will rise. As it reaches 0.6 V, the transistor will turn on.

The resistor R2 has little effect on the voltage at the transistor base, as the current flowing is very small. (See page 119 for clarification of this point.) The purpose of R2 is to limit the current to a safe level, thus protecting the transistor even if VR1 is turned to zero. Resistor R1 does not provide enough protection as its low value is chosen to match the resistance of the LDR in sunlight.

Resistor R3 prevents too much current flowing through the LED when the transistor turns on. Diode D1 is required to short circuit the back e.m.f. produced by the relay. If a relay is not required, D1 may be omitted.

Breadboard construction (Figure 2.11)

1 Fit the wire links as shown.
2 Fit the preset, bending the right hand tag underneath to connect with the correct line of sockets.
3 Fit the resistors.
4 Fit the transistor and LED the correct way round. Diode D1 must be fitted if a relay is used.
5 Fit the LDR and power supply connections.

Stripboard construction (Figure 2.12)

1 Label the stripboard.
2 Fit and solder the preset VR1.
3 Solder in the wire link as indicated.
4 Solder the resistors.
5 Fit the transistor (and optional diode) the correct way round as shown.
6 The LED may be fitted directly to the stripboard, or may be attached with wires. Make sure it is connected the correct way round.
7 Similarly, the light dependent resistor may be soldered to the stripboard or

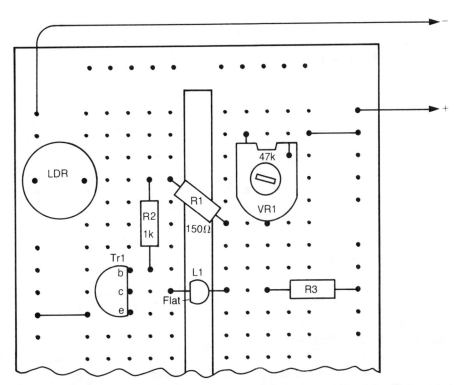

Figure 2.11 Light activated switch: layout diagram for breadboard construction   (Note: There are 2 wire links. D1 is not included.)

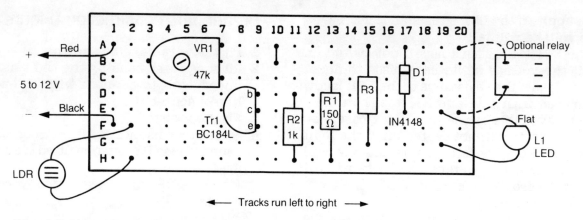

Figure 2.12 Light activated switch: layout diagram for stripboard construction
(Note: D1 is required only if a relay is used. Space is available to mount the LDR and L1 on the stripboard if required.)

attached with wires. It may be connected either way round.

8 Connect the battery clip the correct way round, noting that red is positive.

Testing

(Read the section on 'Fault finding' in Chapter 6.)

Connect the supply the correct way round, and adjust the position of preset VR1 until the LED switches on or off. Now adjust it so that the LED is just off. Reduce the light falling on the LDR by shading it. The LED should now switch on.

If the LED will not switch off, the likely cause is incorrect positioning or a faulty connection around the LDR. If this is not the cause, check that no short-circuit exists (possibly caused by two tracks bridged with solder) in the circuit around the preset. If all else fails, carefully cut one of resistor R2's wires (it will later be joined again with a small blob of solder). The LED should now switch off. If it does not, then the transistor may be faulty (unlikely if new) or a short-circuit may exist near its connections.

If the LED fails to switch on, regardless of the position of VR1, the fault could be almost anywhere. A spare 1k resistor (or similar value) temporarily connected from the positive supply to the transistor base should cause the LED to light. If it does not, then the fault is around the transistor, LED or R3. If the LED does light, then the fault may be associated with VR1, R1, R2 or the LDR.

Extending the circuit

Lighting a LED in this way provides a useful illustration of the use of light dependent resistors, but is of limited practical use. A very worthwhile step is the use of a relay to enable any lamp, motor etc. to be controlled by a change in light level.

Connecting a relay

The relay should be capable of operating on the voltage chosen (see Chapter 1 for coil resistance details). Some relays plug directly into stripboard or p.c.b. – and although convenient, great care must be taken to ensure that each part is connected correctly. Other types have contacts to which are soldered wire connections.

Begin by connecting the diode as indicated in Figure 2.12. Next, connect the relay coil. Any device may now be connected to the relay contacts, wiring them as you would a switch. Note that a second diode is not required to protect the relay contacts – regardless of the device connected. When selecting a relay, the catalogue or advertisement will indicate the maximum voltage and current which the relay contacts can handle. If this is exceeded, the relay contacts may rapidly burn out.

Providing the correct relay is selected – noting its coil voltage, resistance and contacts rating – almost anything can be switched, even mains lights and motors. Hence the circuit can form the basis of a very useful system, turning on lights, drawing curtains etc., as darkness approaches.

Sound to Light Unit

Suitable supply voltage: 5 to 9 V d.c.

Applications

This project will pulse a single LED or a number of LEDs in time with a signal it receives from the speaker output of a radio, record player, tape recorder, etc.

It may also operate from the 'line output' of a tape recorder etc. or, with the addition of a small pre-amplifier circuit (see Chapter 3), a microphone may be used.

Components

Semiconductors
Tr1 transistor BC184L
Tr2 transistor BC184L
D1   diode 1N4148
L1   LED, 10 mA, any size

Resistors (any type)
R1   470 kΩ (yellow, violet, yellow, 'any')
R2   10 kΩ (brown, black, orange, 'any')
R3   390 Ω (orange, white, brown, 'any')
     or 180 Ω (brown, grey, brown, 'any')
     on a 5 V supply
     (If several LEDs are used see text for value of R3)
VR1 preset, min. horizontal, 47 kΩ

Capacitors (16 V or more)
C1   10 μF electrolytic

Miscellaneous
connecting wires/battery clip
stripboard, at least 20 holes by 9 tracks (not BB)

How it works

The loudspeaker output (or line output) from the amplifier of a radio, record player or tape recorder consists of an a.c. signal, the size (amplitude) of which determines the sound level produced. This circuit (Figure 2.13) takes a very small proportion of the signal, amplifies it, and converts it into a pulsing d.c. signal sufficient in strength to drive a LED. The circuit will not affect the amplifier in any way.

An audio signal is an electric current which varies in exact step with the original sound wave which caused it. As before, we will call the negative power supply connection 'zero volts'. The signal output from the amplifier is connected across preset VR1 and the zero volts line. (Note that the zero volts line is sometimes called 'ground' or 'earth', though these terms are not strictly accurate.)

The centre contact of VR1 can sweep from zero volts (no signal) to the maximum signal available from the loudspeaker output. Thus VR1 acts as a **gain** control, allowing the user to compensate for loud or quiet music.

The centre contact of VR1 is connected to capacitor C1. This allows the a.c. audio

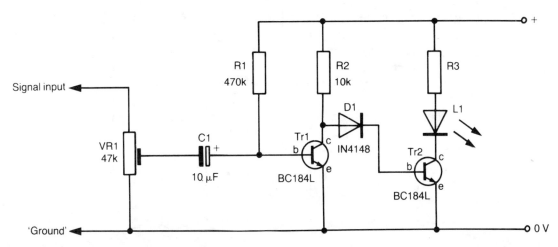

Figure 2.13 Sound to light unit: circuit diagram

signal to flow into the base of transistor Tr1, but prevents the flow of d.c. in either direction. (See the description of capacitors in Chapter 6.) Resistor R1 conducts enough current to allow transistor Tr1 to 'switch on'. Capacitor C1 prevents this current flowing through VR1.

With Tr1 'switched on', the voltage at its collector falls to nearly zero, and Tr2 is switched off. Thus the LED does not light. When an audio signal is also present at the base of Tr1, the signal will cause Tr1 to rapidly switch off and on. Loud sounds, which produce larger (higher amplitude) waves, will cause Tr1 to switch off for a longer period compared with its 'on' time.

When Tr1 switches off, the voltage at its collector rises. Current therefore flows via D1 to the base of Tr2, switching on Tr2 and hence the LED. Thus a large audio signal will cause the LED to appear brighter. Series resistor R3 prevents too much current flowing, should Tr2 turn on fully.

Breadboard construction (Figure 2.14)

1　Fit the wire links as shown
2　Fit the preset VR1, bending its right-hand tag underneath to connect with the correct line of holes.
3　Fit the resistors
4　Fit the diode with the band at the bottom end as shown.
5　Fit the electrolytic capacitor ensuring that the negative side is towards the top of the breadboard.
6　Fit the transistors with the flat sides toward each other.
7　Fit the LED with its flat side facing left.
8　The signal input lead and 'ground' lead may be ordinary insulated wire. Fit these and the supply connections.

Stripboard construction (Figure 2.15)

1　Label the stripboard
2　With the aid of a small drill, or track cutter, break the track as indicated on the copper side.

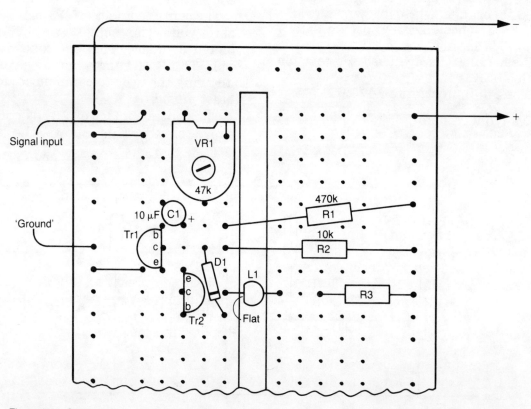

Figure 2.14 Sound to light unit: layout diagram for breadboard construction   (Note: There are 2 wire links.)

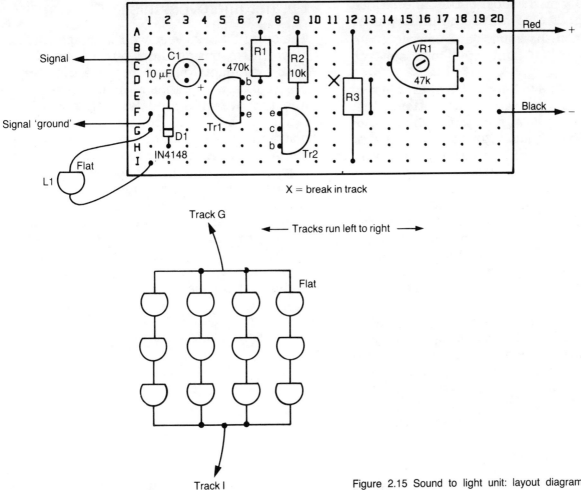

X = break in track

Track G

← Tracks run left to right →

Flat

Track I

Chains of LEDs may be connected like this

Figure 2.15 Sound to light unit: layout diagram for stripboard construction
(Note: There is 1 wire link.)

Please note the importance of fitting components on the correct side of the break in track D. Follow the diagram exactly.

3 Fit and solder preset VR1.
4 Solder in the wire link and resistors.
5 Solder the transistors and capacitor the correct way round.
6 The LED may be fitted directly to the stripboard, or connected via wires. Note that the LED will work only if connected the *correct way round*. If several LEDs are to be used, just fit the wires for now.
7 Connect flexible wires (or a battery clip) for the supply.
8 Ordinary flexible wires may be used for the signal input. Alternatively, to guard against the circuit picking up unwanted signals from nearby electrical equipment (interference — often referred to as elec-

trical 'noise'), screened cable may be used. In this case, the *outer* (screen) connects to 'earth' or 'ground', and the *inner* connection goes to 'signal', as indicated in the diagram.

Testing

(Read the section on 'Fault finding' in Chapter 6.)

Turn the preset to full gain (fully clockwise). Connect the supply. The LED should *not* light up. Connect the two audio signal input wires of the sound to light circuit to the speaker output or line output of the amplifier, and play some loud music. (Further details on connecting to audio equipment are provided on page 65.) The LED should now respond to the music. If it remains fully on for most of the time, reduce the setting of VR1 until the LED pulses correctly with the music (and/or reduce the volume setting if connected to a speaker output).

If the LED fails to light, use a short piece of wire to join the collector and emitter of Tr2 together. (*Do not let this touch the base of Tr2.*) The LED should light up. If it does not, it is probably connected the wrong way round, or on the wrong tracks. Alternatively, R3 may be at fault.

If the LED did light up, use the wire to join the base of Tr1 to the negative side of the power supply. The LED should now light again, showing that Tr1 and nearby components are connected correctly. In this case, the fault must lie around C1, VR1 or the input signal.

If the LED lights up even without an input signal, use a piece of wire to temporarily join the collector and emitter of Tr1. The LED must now go out, unless Tr2, or its nearby tracks, are short-circuiting. If the LED did go out, check R1 carefully and check that the base of Tr1 is not shorting to ground.

Connecting several LEDs

If a 9 V supply is used, up to 3 LEDs may be connected in series, providing that the value of resistor R3 is changed accordingly. Further chains of LEDs may be connected in parallel with the first chain, and the circuit will drive at least 12 LEDs connected as shown in Figure 2.15, providing the correct value of R3 is selected. As a guide, assuming that standard 10 to 15 mA LEDs are used, a series chain of 3 would require a 220 Ω resistor for R3. An array of 12 LEDs connected as shown would require a 68 Ω resistor for R3.

Further improvements

The circuit works very well with speech and slow music, but does not pulse a great deal with fast music. This is because the circuit reacts to a wide range of audio frequencies and the overall sound level in pop music tends to be fairly constant. The simple addition of a capacitor in series with the signal input will tend to block lower frequencies, allowing the circuit to react to higher frequencies only. The required value should be obtained by trial and error, but start with a value of about 0.01 µF (10 nF.). Smaller values will inhibit bass notes to a larger extent, but if the value chosen is too small, the circuit will become too insensitive to all audio frequencies.

Intruder Alarm

Suitable supply voltage: 5 to 12 V d.c.

Applications

This circuit can form the heart of either a simple alarm circuit, for protecting a cupboard or single room, or it can be extended to protect an entire house. With some thought, the circuit may also be adapted to protect a bicycle or car. The project uses very little current when set and, if powered by a battery, the battery should last many months, or even years.

Components

Semiconductors
Th1 thyristor type C106
      (There may be another letter after this code, e.g. C106D. In this circuit this letter is not important.)
Tr1 transistor BC184L
D1   diode 1N4001 or 1N4148 (not BB)

Resistors (any type)
R1   1 kΩ (brown, black, red, 'any')
R2   1 MΩ (brown, black, green, 'any')
R3   10 kΩ (brown, black, orange, 'any')
R4   1 kΩ
R5   10 kΩ
R6   1 kΩ

Capacitors (any type)
C1   0.1 μF
C2   0.1 μF
C3   470 μF electrolytic 16 V or more (not BB)

Miscellaneous
S1   toggle switch or key switch (not BB)
S2   toggle switch or key switch
B1   buzzer, bleeper or siren (see text)
alarm switches (see text)
stripboard, at least 32 holes by 9 tracks (not BB)
battery clip (PP3 or PP9)

Alarm switches

In order to understand the principles of alarm circuits, some knowledge of the types of switches available is helpful. Two main types of switches are used: 'normally open' (off) types, and 'normally closed' (on) types. Normally open switches are more straightforward, but may be disconnected by an intruder without detection by the alarm circuit. Normally closed switches trigger the alarm when they switch off; thus, if the intruder cuts the wires linking the switches, the alarm will be triggered anyway.

Quite an effective alarm system may be designed using magnetic reed switches. These are inexpensive, and consist of two contacts inside a small glass tube. When a magnet is held near the tube, the contacts close (switch on). Thus the reed switch may be fastened to a door frame. The magnet is then fixed to the door so that when the door is closed the magnet causes the switch to close (switch on). As the door opens, the magnet moves away from the reed switch, and the contacts open. In this application the reed switch is therefore normally closed. Popular types of switches are as follows.

Normally open switches: pressure mats (under a carpet), micro-switches.
Normally closed switches: magnetic reed switches (when actuated by a magnet), window foil, micro-switches (using extra n/c contact).

Operating the alarm

The master switch (S1) is normally left on all the time, and only used to switch off the alarm if it happens to be triggered. The 'set switch' (S2) is used to set the alarm when you leave your room, or house. When you return, switch off the 'set switch' before you enter. If the alarm is triggered, switching off the 'set switch' will *not* turn off the alarm.

Note that this circuit does not provide exit or entry delays; you have to set the alarm *after* you leave, and switch it off *before* you return. If triggered, the bleeper or siren will sound until the master switch S1 is switched off (or the battery runs down).

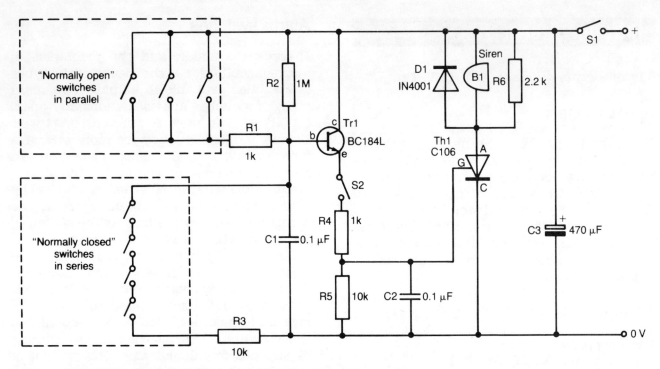

Figure 2.16 Intruder alarm: circuit diagram

How it works

The circuit is shown in Figure 2.16. Assuming that S1 and S2 are switched on, the 'normally open' switches are open, and the 'normally closed' switches are closed, the voltage at the base of transistor Tr1 will be too low to switch Tr1 on. This is because the value of resistor R3 is much lower than R2. Thus no current will flow from the emitter of Tr1.

If one of the 'normally open' switches is closed (by somebody stepping on a pressure mat, for example), the voltage at the base of Tr1 will rise. Alternatively, if any of the 'normally closed' switches are opened (by somebody opening a door, for example), the action of R3 will no longer apply, and again the voltage at the base of Tr1 will rise. Transistor Tr1 will therefore switch on.

Current will then flow via R4 and into the gate of the thyristor. A thyristor is similar to a transistor except that once turned on by current into its gate it will remain on even if the gate current ceases. It will only return to its off state if the current flowing from its anode to its cathode is interrupted. In other words, once the alarm is triggered, it will remain switched on even if the person closes the door etc.

Resistor R5 ensures that the thyristor gate is held at zero volts unless current flows through R4. Resistor R6 ensures that a steady current flows through the thyristor, as some buzzers and bleepers do not conduct continuously – and even the slightest interruption will allow the thyristor to switch off. Diode D1 prevents high voltages from the buzzer or relay coil damaging the thyristor. D1 may be omitted if a 'solid state' buzzer, bleeper or siren is used.

Capacitors C1 and C2 remove any electrical noise which may be picked up by the circuit. This noise will be alternating current (a.c.) and will therefore pass through a capacitor. Without these capacitors, the circuit could be falsely triggered, especially if the wires to the intruder switches pass near the mains supply. Capacitor C3 is a 'decoupling' capacitor which maintains a steady voltage across the circuit.

Once triggered, switching off S2 – the 'set switch' – will not turn off the alarm. The master switch, S1, is for this purpose, and for obvious reasons S1 must be concealed – or out of easy reach.

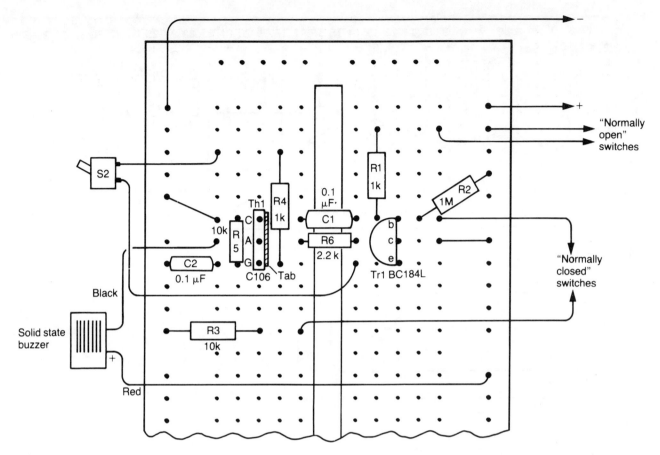

Figure 2.17 Intruder alarm: layout diagram for breadboard construction
(Note: There are 2 wire links.
   D1 has not been included, as the siren would normally be a 'solid state' type.
   S1 and C3 are not included.)

Breadboard construction (Figure 2.17)

Note that the diode D1 is not included, as the buzzer is likely to be a solid state type. If a mechanical buzzer (with a make-and-break contact) or a motor siren is used, D1 should be fitted to protect the thyristor. Capacitor C3 is not required in this 'temporary' circuit.

1 Fit the 2 wire links as shown.
2 Fit the resistors and capacitors.
3 Fit the transistor the correct way round, and likewise the thyristor vertically, with its metal tab towards the right.
4 Fit the solid state buzzer the correct way round.
5 Fit the set switch connections, and the alarm trigger switches connections. A variety of coloured wires will help avoid a muddle. Note that the 'normally closed' switches connections must be joined together if no 'normally closed' switches are required.
6 Fit the supply connections the correct way round.

Stripboard construction (Figure 2.18)

1 Label the stripboard.
2 Solder in the resistors and capacitors, taking care to fit C3 the correct way round.
3 Solder the diode, transistor and thyristor the correct way round.
4 Connect all the flexible wires for the various switches and bleeper or siren.

The circuit should be tested *before* final installation.

Testing

(Read the section on 'Fault finding' in Chapter 6.)

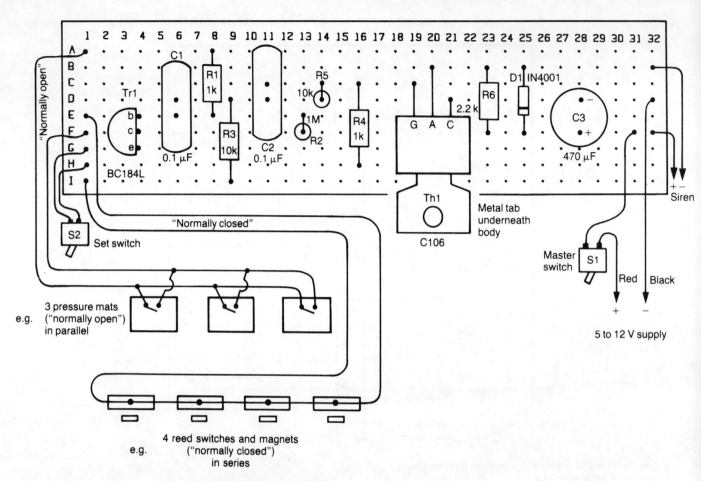

Figure 2.18 Intruder alarm: layout diagram for stripboard construction
Note: If no 'normally closed' switches are used, the wires from tracks E and I must be joined together.)

Twist together the two bare ends of the wires which will eventually connect with the 'normally closed' switches. Leave the 'normally open' wires separated. Switch off S1 and S2.

Connect the power supply. Switch on S1, then S2. Nothing should happen. Touch the bare ends of the 'normally open' wires together. The bleeper should sound. It should continue to sound, even when the 'normally open' wires are moved apart. Switch off S2. The bleeper should still continue to sound.

Switch off S1. The bleeper will stop sounding. Now repeat the test, but instead of touching the 'normally open' leads together, try separating the 'normally closed' leads for a moment. This should also trigger the alarm.

If the circuit fails to work properly, a useful testing point is the gate of the thyristor. Using a spare resistor of about 1 kΩ,

temporarily connect one end to the positive supply, and the other end to the thyristor gate. If this fails to trigger the thyristor and hence the bleeper, then the fault lies in the area of the thyristor. If this test does cause the bleeper to sound, then the fault lies around the transistor.

Siren

Many sounding devices are now available which produce a loud sound, yet consume very little current. These are ideal for this project. The thyristor has a metal tab to which may be attached a piece of metal (known as a heat sink) to conduct away heat. A heat sink should not be necessary in this project, but if in doubt, activate the siren and feel the thyristor to see if it becomes hot. If it becomes too hot to touch, consider using a heat sink, or a more efficient siren. At any rate avoid using a device which consumes more than 1 A (1000 mA).

Using a relay

The alarm may be used to drive a siren or bell of any size, via a relay. In this case connect the relay coil in place of the bleeper, and use its contacts like a switch to operate the siren etc. (See Chapter 1 for details.)

Installation

The master switch S1 and the circuit must be inaccessible to an intruder but within reach — in an emergency — of the occupant. Note that S1 and the circuit need not be in the same place. Providing the alarm is not triggered. S1 can always be left switched on. The current consumption is so small that a 9 V PP9 battery (or 12 V battery) will last many months.

The set switch S2 must be placed where it can be set or turned off by the occupant, without setting off the alarm in the process. It could be concealed just outside the room or house being protected, or alternatively a locking switch (operated by means of a key) could be employed.

Connecting the trigger switches

Any number of either type of trigger switch may be employed. Note that if no 'normally open' switches are required, the 'normally open' wires may be left unconnected. However, if no 'normally closed' switches are needed, the 'normally closed' wires *must* be joined together.

If several 'normally open' switches are used, they must be connected in *parallel*. If several 'normally closed' switches are used, connect them in *series*. (Figure 2.21 should help clarify this and the meaning of 'parallel' and 'series' is explained in Chapter 1.)

3 PROJECTS USING INTEGRATED CIRCUITS

In this chapter, seven projects involving the use of integrated circuits are described. All the projects will work on a 9 V d.c. supply; most will work on 5 V — the exact voltage range is stated in each case.

About the components

Apart from the two voltage regulators, the projects employ a 'dual-in-line' (DIL) integrated circuit (IC). These will plug directly into the breadboard. If using stripboard, always buy an IC socket with the correct number of pins. The integrated circuits all have code numbers. You will often find other letters and numbers printed on the IC apart from the actual code. These should be ignored.

Ensure that you fit an IC the correct way round in a circuit, as described in Chapter 1. Take great care when removing an IC, or you will bend — and possibly damage — its pins. Gently lever it out, using tweezers or a small screwdriver at both ends.

Most of the circuits employ a 'decoupling capacitor'. This helps to ensure a steady voltage supply for the circuit, but in many cases it is not essential and has been omitted from most of the breadboard layouts.

A protective diode is also included in many of the circuits, to guard against connecting a battery incorrectly. This has also been omitted from the breadboard layouts.

Fixed 5 V Regulator

Applications

Provides a 5 V d.c. supply suitable for nearly all the circuits in this book. It may be powered from the d.c. output of a laboratory low-voltage unit, model railway transformer, battery charger, car battery, 9 V battery, etc.

Note: If you wish to solder, construct this circuit on a tag strip, otherwise use a terminal block to avoid soldering.

This simple and inexpensive regulator supplies 5 V at a maximum current of 100 mA. Its input voltage range is from 8 V to about 20 V d.c. It is fully protected against short circuits, overheating and reversed polarity (connecting the input the wrong way round). Since its output current is limited, it will protect many circuits from damage through a variety of causes. It is ideally suited to power 'breadboard circuits' as described in this book, or for testing stripboard circuits before connecting a battery.

A LED indicator is included which should normally be lit. If it goes out, the user is warned of a 'short-circuit' or other serious fault.

As the circuit is so inexpensive and simple to build, a class set could be produced to eliminate damage to circuits caused by excessive voltage etc. Each regulator may be connected to a standard low-voltage unit which may be set to any voltage between 8 and 20 V. Several regulators may be connected to one low-voltage unit if desired.

Alternatively, the regulator may be connected to a centrally controlled low-voltage system, in which case a small switch could be included in each regulator.

Components

Semiconductors
IC1   5 V regulator IC type 78L05
D1   diode 1N4001
L1   LED, about 10 mA, any colour

Resistor (any type)
R1   330 Ω (orange, orange, brown, 'any')

Capacitors (25 V or more)
C1   470 μF electrolytic
C2   0.01 μF (10 nF) disc ceramic

Miscellaneous
tag strip containing 6 tags *or* 6 way terminal
    block
wires
suitable plugs and crocodile clips as required
    (see text)
small plastic case (about 3 by 2 by 1 inches,
    or 75 by 50 by 28 mm)

How it works

The heart of the circuit (Figure 3.1) is the 5 V regulator type 78L05. This amazing little integrated circuit cannot be damaged by short-circuits or any type of overload. The short-circuit current is limited, thus protecting the circuit it is powering, and should the regulator become too hot it will automatically shut down until cool enough to operate again.

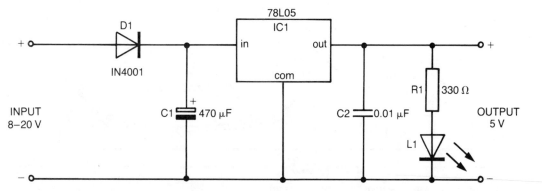

Figure 3.1 Fixed 5 V regulator: circuit diagram

Current from a power supply is fed via diode D1, which protects the circuit, particularly the capacitor, in case the user connects the regulator to the supply the wrong way round, or to an a.c. supply by mistake. The capacitor C1 decouples the supply and provides a steady voltage level for the IC.

The IC is able to accept a voltage from about 7 V to 30 V at its input connection (in). It supplies a steady and very accurate 5.V at its output (out). Its common connection (com) is connected to the zero volts (i.e. negative) line.

The LED L1 will light up when all is well. Should a short circuit develop across the output, L1 will turn off. The resistor R1 is needed to prevent too much current flowing through L1. Capacitor C2 removes any voltage 'spikes' left on the output. If C1 has a working voltage of 25 V, the maximum voltage which may be applied to the regulator input is about 20 V.

Construction (Figure 3.2)

This circuit may be built on stripboard, but the use of a tag strip enables less experienced solderers to tackle the project with confidence. Alternatively, a terminal block may be used, thus avoiding the need for soldering altogether (Figure 3.3).

1 Place insulation over the leads as shown to prevent them touching other metal parts. Insulation may be bought, or stripped from electrical wires. Alternatively insulating tape may be used.
2 Solder (or screw in, if using a terminal block) the wire link and all the components except the LED. Note that IC1 is shown with its leads *toward* you. Ensure that this, D1, and C1 are connected the correct way round.
3 Cut off the surplus wire.
4 Connect the input and output wires; red for positive and black for negative.
5 Plugs may be fitted to the input wires *after they are pushed through the hole in the case.* Likewise, miniature insulated crocodile clips may be fitted to the output wires.
6 Drill four holes in the case: one at each end for the wires, one for the LED (L1) and one for mounting the tag strip (or terminal block).
7 Fix the tag strip (or terminal block) and push the LED into the hole in the case, then solder (or screw in) the leads from the LED the correct way round. Be careful not to touch the plastic case with your soldering iron.

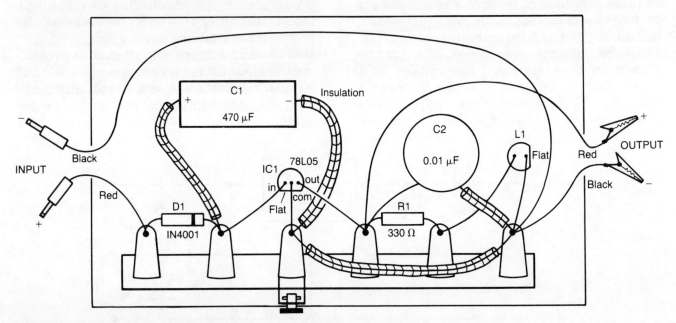

Figure 3.2 Fixed 5 V regulator: layout diagram for tag strip construction
(Note: IC1 is viewed with its leads coming towards you. Use red and black flexible leads for input and output.)

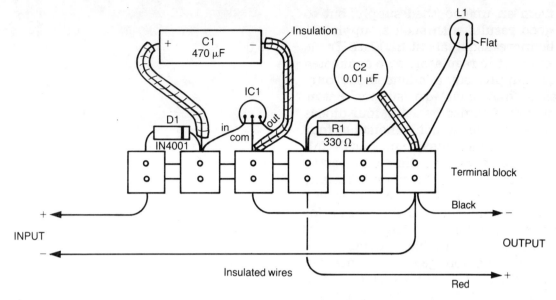

Figure 3.3 Fixed 5 V regulator: layout diagram for terminal block construction
(Note: IC1 is viewed with its leads coming towards you.)

Testing

Note that any voltage from 8 to 20 V d.c. may be used for testing, but voltages at the lower end of the range will do less damage if the circuit has been wired incorrectly. A 9 V battery may be used if desired.

Connect the input to a supply of at least 8 V d.c. The LED should light up. If it does not, disconnect and check for faults. Otherwise connect a voltmeter to the output. It should read 5 V.

Create a short-circuit by touching together the output wires. (Note that if you are using a battery for the supply, this test will soon run it down – be quick!). The LED should go out. If an ammeter is available, set it to 500 mA or more and check the short-circuit current by connecting it across the output. The reading should show an initial surge which may be more than 100 mA, quickly falling to about 100 mA or less.

Fault finding

(Read the section on 'Fault finding' in Chapter 6.)

If the LED fails to light, check the output voltage. If a 5 V reading is obtained, the LED is probably connected the wrong way round or faulty in some other way. Check that R1 is connected to it correctly.

If no output voltage is obtained, check the voltage from the 'in' connection to negative. This should be nearly equal to the supply voltage. If not, check that D1 is connected the correct way round.

Check that C1 is fitted the correct way round, and check all the connections for accuracy and proper joints. Check that the flat edge of the IC is as shown in the diagram, with its leads *toward* you. An output of more than 5.5 V may indicate that the IC is connected the wrong way round.

Using the regulator

Once correctly wired, the regulator will quickly earn its keep in protecting your components against common wiring faults and short-circuits. It is particularly useful for testing newly constructed circuits – even those intended for battery power. It should not be connected to a battery for long periods however, as it uses several milli-amps even when not driving another circuit. If long-term battery use is required, disconnecting the LED will considerably reduce this wasted current.

Variations

The regulator is intended for fairly smooth d.c. supplies. It may produce a satisfactory output from an unsmoothed supply, but to ensure good results with such a supply, C1 should be increased to about 2200 µF. Diode D1 will enable the regulator to be connected to an a.c. supply, but a single diode only produces a 'half wave' d.c. supply. Better results will be obtained by using four diodes (or a bridge rectifier which consists of four diodes in a single package), to produce a 'full wave' supply, as shown in the next circuit.

The regulator type 78L05 is one of many types of fixed voltage regulator. Other voltages are available, such as the 78L12 for 12 V or the 78L15 for 15 V. Higher current regulators are also available, providing 1 A, 5 A etc. at various voltages. Note, however, that these higher current regulators will provide far less protection for your delicate circuits!

Variable voltage regulators are also available, and such a device is the subject of the next project to be described.

Variable Voltage Regulator

It is unlikely that you will wish to construct this circuit in a temporary way, and only a stripboard version is described.

Many people have some type of fixed voltage mains power unit, such as a model railway 'transformer', battery charger, computer power supply, etc. These power units provide a 'nominal' output voltage. The word 'nominal' indicates that the voltage is very approximate. For example, a 12 V model railway transformer may produce about 15 V when 'off load' (not connected to a motor).

The previous regulator provided a fixed 5 V supply. This more complicated circuit provides a variable supply. It will handle any input voltage to a maximum of 20 V d.c. or 15 V a.c. and will produce a regulated output voltage from 1.2 V to about 12 V.

If an a.c. source is used, the conversion from a.c. to d.c. which takes place in this circuit results in a voltage increase of about 1.4 times. Thus a 15 V a.c. supply will increase to about 21 V d.c.

The voltage regulator will also remove any ripples or irregularities in the supply. It can even be connected to the electrical supply of a car, despite the electrical noise produced by the engine and generator.

The regulator may be connected either way round to a battery or d.c. power unit, or to an alternating current (a.c.) supply.

Components

Semiconductors
IC1 variable regulator type LM317M (or LM317T) (see text)
Tr1 transistor BC184L
D1 diode 1N4001 (or 1N5400)
D2 diode 1N4001 (or 1N5400)
D3 diode 1N4001 (or 1N5400)
D4 diode 1N4001 (or 1N5400)
L1 LED, about 10 mA, any colour
use the diodes in brackets if using regulator type LM317T

Resistors (in each case, the fourth band should be gold, red or brown)
R1 1.5 kΩ (brown, green, red)
R2 430 Ω (yellow, orange, brown)
R3 4.7 kΩ (yellow, violet, red)
R4 10 kΩ (brown, black, orange)
VR1 potentiometer, 5 kΩ (or 4.7 kΩ) linear

Capacitors (all 25 V or more)
C1 1000 μF electrolytic
C2 0.1 μF any type
C3 1 μF electrolytic

Miscellaneous
S1 switch (any type)
knob for VR1
L.V. sockets (for output)
stripboard 7 cm by 4 cm (at least 20 holes by 9 tracks)
heat sink (see text)
case
insulated connecting wire

How it works

Providing a regulated voltage supply is much more difficult than it may sound. A full understanding of Ohm's Law (see page 117) will indicate that voltage depends upon resistance *and* current. Thus if you wish, for example, to reduce 12 V to 9 V, a simple resistor may be used *providing* a known current flows. Most electronic circuits do not consume a constant current and this method therefore provides a very unpredictable voltage.

The Variable Regulator Integrated Circuit type LM317M or LM317T is a complete electronic circuit contained in a chip of silicon and housed in a small piece of plastic with three leads, rather like some power transistors. It is able to maintain a steady output voltage to within a fraction of a volt, even when the output current varies. If the current exceeds the maximum permitted, the integrated circuit (IC) limits the current by reducing the output voltage. Thus a 'short-circuit' will not damage the IC in any way. Thermal shutdown is also included, whereby the IC automatically 'shuts down' if it becomes too hot. Altogether a very clever chip!

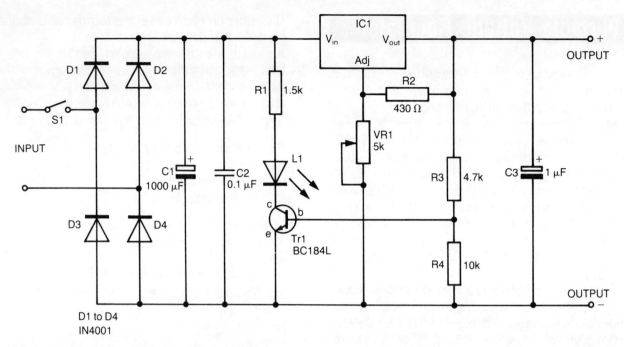

Figure 3.4 Variable voltage regulator: circuit diagram

The maximum current supplied is either 0.5 A from the LM317M type, or 1.5 A from the LM317T type. The LM317M version will offer more protection to circuits which require less than 500 mA, since the 'short-circuit' output current is limited to about 1 A. The LM317T version will provide any current up to 1500 mA. It is therefore more versatile, but offers less protection since the 'short-circuit' current is over 2 A.

Either type of IC may be used with an input of up to 39 V. In this circuit, however, the maximum input voltage permitted is 20 V, since capacitor C1 (and possibly C3) is rated at 25 V. A higher voltage capacitor could be used, but it should be noted that the heat produced by the IC will be much greater at higher voltages, and the heat sink may have to be increased in size.

As indicated in Figure 3.4, the integrated circuit has only three pins: Voltage in (V_{in}), Voltage out (V_{out}) and 'Adj'. The 'Adj' lead employs a variable resistor to control the output voltage.

The complete circuit adds several refinements to the basic function of the IC. S1 is an on/off switch, and diodes D1 to D4 form a 'bridge rectifier' which ensures that the circuit functions correctly regardless of which way round the supply is connected.

The bridge rectifier will also convert an alternating current (a.c.) to direct current (d.c.), making the project very versatile.

These diodes may be omitted if you intend to use only a d.c. supply, and if care is taken to connect the supply the correct way round. In this case the positive input must go to track 'A', and the negative to track 'I' on the stripboard.

Capacitor C1 is a smoothing capacitor which provides a reasonably steady voltage for the IC. Large-value capacitors are not able to smooth very fast electrical ripples, such as high-voltage spikes which sometimes appear on the supply. Therefore a small capacitor C2 is connected in parallel with C1 to meet this requirement.

The cost of the project is reduced by not including a voltmeter to monitor the output. This can pose problems. For example, if a device being powered by the regulator contains a 'short circuit', no indication is provided for the user. The problem is overcome by the addition of an inexpensive circuit comprising R1, L1, Tr1, R3, and R4, which provides a visual indication of a fault. When operating normally, the LED (L1) will glow. If too much current is used from the regulator — as happens when a short circuit occurs — the LED will stop glowing.

The resistors R3 and R4 form a 'potential divider'. This means that the output voltage is reduced by about one-third at the base of Tr1. Even at the lowest output voltage setting of 1.2 V, the voltage present at the base of Tr1 will be at least 0.6 V, and sufficient current will flow into the base to hold Tr1 on. Thus L1 will glow. However, if too much current flows from the output (caused by a 'short circuit' for example) the voltage at the output will fall to near zero, thus reducing the voltage at the base of Tr1 to less than 0.6 V. Tr1 therefore switches off, and L1 stops glowing.

When the regulator is used to power an electronic project, L1 should always glow. If it stops glowing, a fault (probably a 'short circuit') exists in the project being powered; if S1 is turned off immediately, no damage should occur to the project being powered. No damage will occur in the regulator itself, as the IC is fully self protecting as described previously.

If the LED L1 is not required, R1, L1, Tr1, R3 and R4 may all be omitted.

Voltage control is provided by means of variable resistor VR1. This varies the current flowing from the 'Adj' pin of the IC, and allows the IC to control its output voltage.

Construction

The majority of components are housed on a piece of stripboard of at least 20 holes by 9 tracks. A larger piece of stripboard may be preferred, to allow four mounting holes to be drilled.

1 Begin by marking out the stripboard in the usual way, with the tracks running left to right.
2 Assemble the components, taking care to fit the transistor, electrolytic capacitors and diodes the correct way round.
3 The regulator IC (IC1) is positioned in order to allow a heat sink to be fitted. A

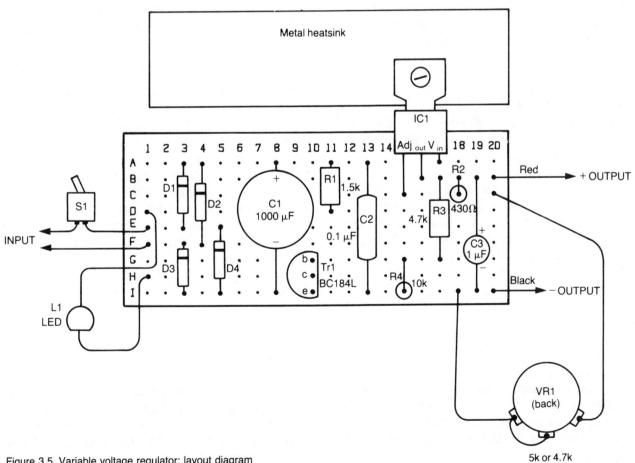

Figure 3.5 Variable voltage regulator: layout diagram

heat sink is a piece of metal which rapidly conducts heat away from the IC. The heat sink is not critical in this project, and a piece of aluminium, copper or steel may be used. Suitable aluminium or copper sheets may be purchased from an electronics supplier; alternatively, sheets of steel may be obtained by cutting up an old 'tin' can. As the steel is rather thin, several sheets should be placed together.

The metal heat sink should measure about 20 cm by 5 cm, though the exact size is not critical. An ineffective heat sink will not damage the IC in any way; if the IC becomes too hot, it will simply 'shut down' until cool enough to operate again.

If the project is to be housed in a metal case, the case itself could be used as the heat sink. Note however, that the metal tab of the IC is internally connected to the 'V_{out}' pin, and must *not* be directly connected to the metal case. Special insulating washers are available which will sandwich between the metal tab of the IC and the case. These allow the heat to pass, but prevent any electricity flowing from the tab into the case. A small insulating washer is also required to prevent the securing screw conducting current from the tab to the case. Alternatively, nylon nuts and bolts are available.

4 The LED (L1) is connected via flexible wires, so that it may be mounted on the case. Ensure that it is connected the correct way round. Flexible wires are also used to connect the potentiometer and output terminals. Any type of terminal may be employed, and some firms stock 'L.V. sockets' which provide a particularly neat finish. Note that red should be used to indicate positive (+), and black for negative (−). The input may also be via terminals, or a twin flex lead. Since it does not matter which way round the input is connected, input colours are not important.

5 The completed circuit should be housed in a metal or plastic case. A wide variety of cases is available from electronics suppliers. Take care to allow sufficient space for the heat sink, and allow clearance for VR1 and S1.

Drill the various holes required for S1, VR1, LP1 and the stripboard mounting bolts. A few extra ventilation holes should be drilled to allow the air to circulate, especially near the heat sink.

When fixing the stripboard, ensure that the tracks and solder blobs do not touch the case if it is made of metal. Whether a metal or plastic case is used, it is a good idea to raise the stripboard slightly using small rubber feet, grommets or one of the special p.c.b. mounting aids made for the purpose. A small hole should be drilled in the heat sink to enable fixing to IC1. The circuit should be tested *without* the heat sink in place; if there is a wiring fault, it is much easier to correct if the heat sink is not attached.

Testing

A battery of between 9 and 18 V may be used for testing, but the 'short-circuit' test described later must be done carefully and quickly, otherwise the battery will run down. A better alternative is to use a power unit of some sort, as described earlier.

Turn the potentiometer VR1 to its minimum value (fully anticlockwise when viewed from the front). Connect the input to the battery or power unit. Switch on the regulator. The LED should light. If it does not, quickly switch off and check the diodes for overheating. If they feel warm, there is a 'short-circuit' somewhere on the stripboard or another serious fault.

Assuming all is well, use a voltmeter, bulb, etc. to check the output from the regulator. As VR1 is advanced, the output voltage should rise.

Momentarily short-circuit the output, by joining the positive and negative terminals. The LED should go out, regardless of the setting of VR1.

Calibration

A voltmeter is essential if accurate calibration is required. Calibration involves marking a scale on the case of the regulator, so that a pointer knob fixed to VR1 may be used to indicate the voltage set.

Connect the voltmeter to the output terminals. Set VR1 to its minimum value. The voltmeter should read 1.2 V. Decide which voltages you would like to mark on the scale. Useful settings are 3 V, 5 V, 9 V and 12 V. Use the voltmeter to determine the position of the pointer knob at these voltages, and mark a scale accordingly. A variety of marker pens may be employed for this task, or small transfer numbers may be purchased from electronics suppliers or stationery shops.

Fault finding

(Read the section on 'Fault finding' in Chapter 6.)

Assuming that a voltmeter is available, simple voltage readings around the circuit should quickly uncover any faults. If neither the LED nor the output voltage are working correctly, check the voltage between track A (+) and track I (−). This should be nearly equal to the supply voltage. If it is not, then the fault probably lies in S1, or the diodes or input connections.

All the following voltage readings are 'with respect to ground'. In other words, plug the negative lead of the voltmeter into the negative output terminal.

Again check the voltage on track A (i.e. touch the positive lead of the voltmeter on track A). The same reading should be obtained as in the previous test. This proves that the negative output terminal is joined correctly.

Now check the voltage on the 'V_{in}' lead of the IC. The voltage reading should still be the same. Check the voltage on the 'Adj' lead. This should be at zero with VR1 turned fully one way, and rise to several volts with VR1 turned fully the other way. If this is not the case, check R2 and VR1 and their connections carefully.

Odd voltage readings on the 'Adj' lead may also be caused by a 'short-circuit' at the output. Check the voltage on the 'V_{out}' lead. If this is zero, a 'short-circuit' may exist in the region of track B.

If the output works correctly but the LED fails to light, check the voltage on the base of Tr1. It should be more than 0.6 V. If it is not, check R3 and R4 carefully. Otherwise check that Tr1 is correctly fitted and measure the voltage at its collector. This should be nearly zero; if it is not, Tr1 is at fault. A zero collector voltage indicates that the LED or R1 must be at fault.

Electronic Timer

Suitable supply voltage: 5 to 9 V d.c.

Applications

Egg timer, general kitchen timer, pocket reminder etc.

This circuit is based on a very popular integrated circuit type NE555V, sometimes simply called a '555 timer'. A CMOS low-power version is also available, but beginners are recommended to use the standard bipolar version in this circuit, to begin with at least.

Components

Semiconductors
IC1   timer IC type NE555V (or CMOS 555 version ICM 7555)
D1   diode 1N4001 (not BB)

Resistors (any type)
R1   1 kΩ (brown, black, red, 'any')
R2   100 kΩ (brown, black, yellow, 'any')
VR1   potentiometer 1 MΩ linear (not BB) (a 1 MΩ sub min. horizontal preset is suggested for breadboard layouts)

Capacitors (all 16 V or more)
C1   1000 µF electrolytic
C2   0.01 µF any type (not BB)
C3   0.1 µF any type
C4   0.1 µF any type
C5   47 µF electrolytic (not BB)

Miscellaneous
B1   solid state buzzer (6 V)
S1   toggle switch (any type)
IC socket, 8 pin DIL (not BB)
PP3 battery clip
knob for VR1 (not BB)
stripboard (0.1 in pitch) 7 cm by 3 cm (not BB) (at least 26 holes by 8 tracks)
case (not BB)
insulated connecting wire
bare wire (tinned copper) for links (24 SWG approx.)

The NE555V timer

The NE555 timer IC is a very stable, reliable and, above all, cheap device which may be used as a **monostable** to time periods from a fraction of a second up to an hour. In the circuit described, times from about one second to 20 minutes are provided, though this may be increased as explained later. The time required is set by a potentiometer, VR1. The timer is then switched on and after the required period a 'bleep' occurs until switched off again (Figure 3.6).

As indicated in the pin out diagram (Figure 3.7), pin 1 of the NE555 IC is connected to 'ground' (the negative of the battery in this case).

Pin 2 is the 'trigger', and causes the IC to begin timing upon the receipt of a 'negative' pulse.

The output is taken from pin 3. Before the IC begins timing, the output pin is at zero volts. Once triggered, the voltage at pin 3 rises to nearly the supply voltage for the time period set, falling to zero again at the end of that period. Figures 3.8 and 3.9 show alternative ways of connecting a buzzer or light, depending on whether you wish the buzzer to sound during the timing period, or after the timing period. In this circuit the buzzer is wired from positive to pin 3. Thus it is silent during the timing period, but switches on at the end of that period. A maximum current of 200 mA may be allowed to flow to or from pin 3 of the normal (bipolar) NE555 IC. This figure is 100 mA in the CMOS version.

Pin 4 provides a 'reset' facility. A negative pulse at pin 4 will cause the IC to reset. This is not required here, and is connected to the positive supply to avoid the timer resetting accidentally.

The voltage at pin 5 affects, to a small extent, the time period. A variable resistor could be used to control this voltage, but a much larger range of control is provided at pin 6. In most circuits, therefore, pin 5 is connected to 'ground' via a small capacitor. This 'decouples' (provides a more steady voltage for) the IC, resulting in more reliable operation. Note that this capacitor is

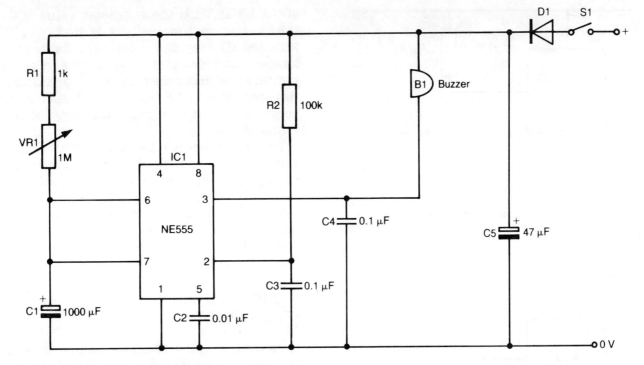

Figure 3.6 Electronic timer: circuit diagram

unnecessary if a CMOS version of the IC is used, though it may be retained if preferred.

When the voltage at pin 6 rises to two-thirds of the supply voltage (this is known as the 'threshold'), the timing period ends and the output voltage at pin 3 falls to zero. The method by which this occurs will become clear later.

At the end of the timing period, pin 7 rapidly discharges the timing capacitor — also explained later.

Pin 8 is connected to the positive supply and is the source of power for the IC.

How it works

It will be obvious from the description above that pins 8 and 4 must be connected to the positive supply. Pin 1 is connected to zero volts, and C2 'decouples' the IC at pin 5 (Figure 3.6).

When switch S1 is closed (switched on), current flows via diode D1 into the IC. The purpose of D1 is to prevent damage to the circuit if the battery is connected the wrong way round. At the moment of switching on, the voltage at pin 2 will be zero. This zero voltage will act like a negative pulse and trigger the IC. Thus the timing period will

begin. Within a fraction of a second enough current will have passed through resistor R2 to charge capacitor C3 to the supply voltage. The IC will not work properly if the trigger input is allowed to remain at zero volts.

The flow of current through resistors R1 and VR1 slowly charges up capacitor C1. The rate of flow of current is controlled by the setting of VR1. R1 is a safety device to prevent the large flow of current which will occur if VR1 is set to zero resistance. The voltage on C1 and hence pin 6 of the IC slowly rises until the threshold is reached. The time this takes depends upon the flow of current and therefore the setting of VR1.

Before the threshold is reached, the output voltage at pin 3 is nearly equal to the supply

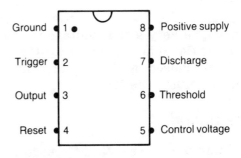

Figure 3.7 Pin out diagram of the NE555V IC

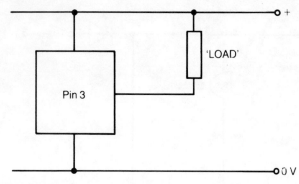

Figure 3.8 NE555 timer: output acting as a 'sink' – as used in the circuit diagram (Figure 3.6). At switch on, timer is activated, output goes 'high' and no current flows through 'load'. At end of time period, output goes 'low', and current flows from positive, through 'load'.

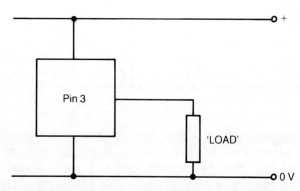

Figure 3.9 NE555 timer: output acting as a 'source'. At switch on, timer is activated, output goes 'high' and current flows through 'load' to 'zero volts line'. At end of time period, output goes 'low' and current no longer flows through 'load'.

voltage. Thus the buzzer will not sound as both its connections are at the same voltage. The moment the threshold voltage is reached at pin 6, the IC causes the voltage at pin 3 to fall to zero and the buzzer sounds. At this moment pin 7 discharges the capacitor (i.e. rapidly reduces the voltage to zero) ready for the next timing operation. The buzzer will continue to sound until S1 is turned off.

Capacitor C5 'decouples' the supply (i.e. maintains a very steady voltage for the IC). Capacitor C4 removes any irregular 'spikes' of voltage caused by the buzzer, which may otherwise upset the IC.

Time period

The maximum resistance recommended between the positive supply and pin 6 is about 1 MΩ. With the suggested value of C1, the maximum time setting is just over 20 minutes. C1 may be increased in value for a longer time delay, but larger values will produce less accurate results. The maximum time period may be reduced by reducing the value of C1. In this case, accuracy should increase.

There is a direct relationship between the size of capacitor C1 and the time period. For example, if the capacitor is doubled to 2200 μF (the nearest available value), the maximum time increases to about 40 minutes. Halving the capacitor to 470 μF. (nearest value), will reduce the maximum time to about 10 minutes.

Breadboard construction (Figure 3.10)

Note that D1, C2 and C5 are not required in this temporary layout.

1 Fit the IC the correct way round. Be careful not to bend the pins – ease them gently into position. If the IC has to be removed, see the note at the beginning of this chapter.
2 Fit the wire links.
3 Fit VR1 and the other components, with C1 the correct way round.
4 Fit the buzzer leads and the supply leads the correct way round.

Stripboard construction (Figure 3.11)

1 Mark the board as usual with the tracks running left to right. Mark the positions of the breaks.
2 Break the tracks between the pins of the IC holder as shown.
3 Solder in the IC holder, followed by the wire links.
4 Solder in the remaining components, noting that the diode and electrolytic capacitors must be connected the correct way round.
5 Solder in the wires joining the buzzer, potentiometer, toggle switch and battery clip.
6 Finally plug in the NE555 IC the correct way round.

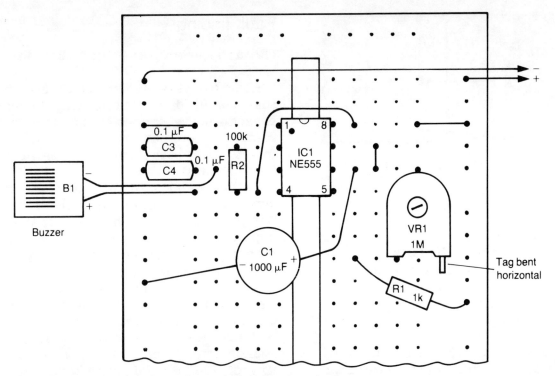

Figure 3.10 Electronic timer: layout diagram for breadboard construction
(Note: There are 4 wire links.
    A preset is used for VR1 in place of the potentiometer.
    D1, C1 and C5 are not included.)

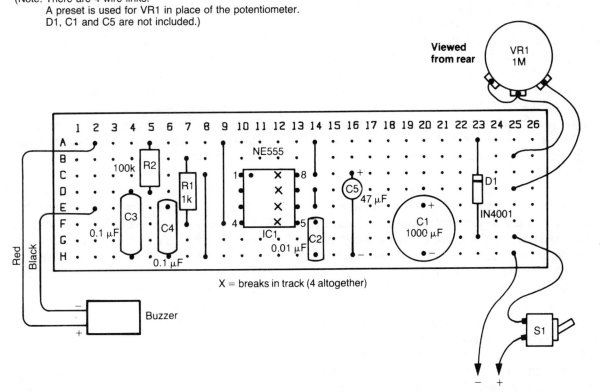

X = breaks in track (4 altogether)

Figure 3.11 Electronic timer: layout diagram for stripboard construction
(Note: There are 4 wire links.)

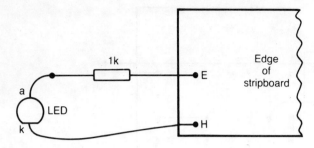

Figure 3.12 Diagram showing how the output from the NE555 timer may be connected as a source to light a LED while the timer is active.
(Note: The 'load' is composed of the LED and series resistor)

Connecting an LED
Figure 3.12 shows how the buzzer may be replaced with an LED and a series resistor if preferred.

Setting up and testing

Set the potentiometer VR1 to its minimum value (fully anticlockwise when viewed from the front – if wired correctly). Switch on S1. After a very short delay of a second or less, the buzzer should sound. Switch off S1. Advance the setting of VR1 by a very short distance. Switch on S1 again; after a slightly longer time, the buzzer should sound. If all is well, advance VR1 fully. The time delay should now be over 20 minutes.

If a preset is used for VR1, it is not possible to calibrate a time scale, and the next two paragraphs may be disregarded.

Calibrating VR1 involves marking out a scale in minutes from 0 to 20. Clearly this can only be accomplished when the timer circuit is in a case. The potentiometer must be mounted so that a control knob may be fixed outside the case. It may be necessary to reduce the length of VR1's spindle, using a small hacksaw or even a pair of tin snips.

The scale must be calibrated by trial and error. Begin by finding the exact five minute point. The ten minute setting will be at roughly twice this distance from zero, the fifteen minute setting at three times the distance, and so on. Estimate each point, then check it for accuracy before marking it.

Fault finding

(Read the section on 'Fault finding' in Chapter 6.)

Apart from the usual visual checks, ensure that the IC, diode, buzzer and electrolytic capacitors are connected the correct way round. A common stripboard mistake is forgetting to break the tracks between the pins of the IC.

If the buzzer still fails to work at all, switch on S1 and check the voltage from pin 8 to pin 1 of the IC. It should be at about the supply voltage. Check the voltage between output pin 3 and 'ground'. During timing this should be nearly equal to the supply; at the end of the timing period it should fall to nearly zero volts. If the output responds correctly, the fault lies in the buzzer.

If the buzzer still fails to work, or if it sounds continuously regardless of the setting of VR1, the following tests may help trace the fault. Check the voltage from pin 4 to 'ground'. It should be at about the supply. Check the voltage from pin 2 to ground. It should be more than half the supply voltage, otherwise R2 may be at fault. Try momentarily shorting pin 2 to ground with a piece of wire. If the timer now works, the fault lies in C3 or its connections.

To check the charging up of capacitor C1, a voltmeter should be connected from pin 6 or 7 (the readings on both pins should be identical) to 'ground'. Set potentiometer VR1 to its minimum value (fully anticlockwise when viewed from the front). Switch on S1. The voltage should quickly rise to several volts as C1 charges up. Now set VR1 to its maximum value. Switch on S1. This time the voltage should remain at nearly zero. In theory the voltage will rise very slowly, as C1 charges, but in practice the current used by the voltmeter may prevent this happening.

Using a CMOS IC

A CMOS version of the 555 timer is available and is sometimes coded ICM 7555. It has the considerable advantage of using a fraction of the current used by the bipolar 555 timer during the timing period. Thus the battery will last much longer. The CMOS version is more expensive, and can only provide 100.mA at output pin 3. This is more than enough for the buzzer specified. CMOS ICs should normally be handled with caution, but the 7555 version is fairly well protected against static electricity from your fingers and no handling precautions should be necessary.

The CMOS timer IC may be directly substituted for the bipolar type. The spare bipolar 555 timer will be useful for the next circuit.

Electronic Organ

Suitable supply voltage: 5 to 12 V d.c.

Applications

This type of simple electronic organ is able to play a wide range of single notes. Proper piano keys could be used, but since only single notes are possible, the simplest method of construction involves the use of a 'stylus'. This may be constructed from an old pen – as described later – which is used to 'touch' the required note.

The organ may be linked to the 'Sound to light unit' (page 23) if desired.

Components

Semiconductors
IC1   NE555V timer IC (or CMOS version)
D1   diode 1N4001 (not BB)

Resistors (any type)
R1   10 kΩ (brown, black, orange, 'any')
R2   12 kΩ (brown, red, orange, 'any')
VR1 to VR8 presets 100 kΩ (see note below) (only 2 demonstration presets are included on breadboard)

Capacitors (all 16 V or more)
C1 0.022 µF any type
C2 100 µF electrolytic
C3 100 µF electrolytic

Miscellaneous
S1   on/off switch (any type)
SP1 speaker (see note below)
stripboard 0.1 in pitch, about 6 cm by 3 cm (not BB) (at least 22 holes by 9 tracks)
IC socket, 8 pin DIL (not BB)
PP3 battery clip
wood to house 'notes' (see 'stripboard construction') (not BB)
strips of metal foil (see 'stripboard construction') (not BB)
drawing pins (one for each 'note') (not BB)
insulated connecting wire
bare wire (tinned copper) for links (24 SWG approx.)

Note
The presets may be of any convenient type. At least eight are required (for one octave), but extra presets (for extra notes) will be useful. In view of the large number required, select the least expensive type. The loudspeaker must have an impedance of 50 Ω or more. A telephone type earpiece may be substituted if desired. If a speaker or earpiece of less than 50 Ω impedance is employed, the IC may become hot. In this event, a resistor of about 47 Ω may be wired in series with the speaker or earpiece. (See Figure 3.17.)

How it works

Like the last circuit, this simple electronic organ is based on the NE555V integrated circuit. The circuit is therefore very similar, except that the 'time delay period' is very short, and the IC automatically re-triggers at the end of each 'period'.

When used in this way, the IC is said to be in an **astable** mode of operation. Thus the output voltage 'oscillates' (rises and falls). This, in conjunction with C2, produces an alternating current (a.c.). However, unlike 'mains a.c.' which starts, stops and reverses smoothly, the output from the 555 IC changes very abruptly. This output is called a **square wave**. Mains a.c. on the other hand is a **sine wave** (see Figure 3.14).

A sine wave produces a rather feeble – if pure – sound when fed through a loudspeaker. A musician's tuning fork also produces a sine wave. A square wave produces a much harsher and more interesting sound.

To understand how the IC produces an alternating voltage, it should be noted that the following takes place within a fraction of a second. Assuming that the 'stylus' is touching one of the notes (metal strips in this case), electricity will flow from positive, through resistor R1 (see Figure 3.13), and through one of the preset resistors. To start with, the discharge pin 7 will have no effect since it is 'open circuit' (i.e. disconnected

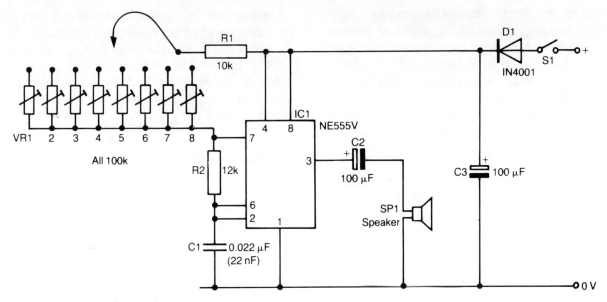

Figure 3.13 Electronic organ: circuit diagram

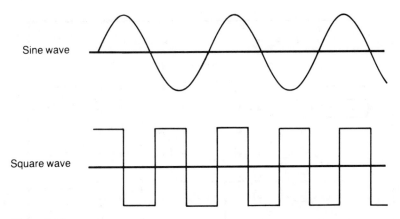

Sine wave

Square wave

Figure 3.14

internally), and the tiny current will continue through R2 and begin to charge capacitor C1. Note that the output pin 3 is positive during this stage.

The voltage on C1 therefore rises, and when the 'threshold voltage' at pin 6 is reached the output pin 3 changes state from positive to zero. In addition, pin 7, the discharge pin, drops to zero volts. The capacitor C1 therefore discharges (loses its charge) via resistor R2. This resistor limits the discharging current, to create a slight delay before the next stage.

The trigger pin 2 activates the IC as its voltage falls to zero. As the voltage on C1 and hence pin 2 falls, the IC is triggered again. The discharge at pin 7 ceases as pin 7 goes 'open circuit' again; output pin 3 changes

state to positive again, and the flow of current via R1, the preset and R2, once again charges up capacitor C1.

The whole process repeats rapidly, with the output at pin 3 constantly changing state. This output may be fed directly to a loudspeaker or earpiece, but a fairly large current will flow when the output goes positive. Such a large flow of d.c. is best avoided, and the purpose of capacitor C2 is to block the d.c. flow, whilst allowing the passage of a.c. (See the description of 'capacitors' in Chapter 6 for clarification of this point.) The net result is that the loudspeaker cone pulses evenly about its mid point, and much less current flows.

The rate at which capacitor C1 charges and discharges determines the frequency of the output. The charge/discharge rate depends upon the size of C1, and the values of R1, R2 and the preset resistor in the circuit. If any of the resistors, or capacitor C1, are reduced in value, then C1 will charge more quickly.

Thus the **frequency** (number of output voltage rises per second) at pin 3 is determined by R1, R2, C1 and the preset resistor in the circuit. Very wide variations are possible, from single 'clicks' to frequencies above the human hearing range. The values suggested offer a medium range of notes, but it may be worth experimenting with other values as well.

The preset resistors allow a fairly wide range of variation so that each preset may be 'tuned' to a different note. R1 is not strictly necessary, but is included in case any of the presets are set to zero ohms — a situation which could otherwise cause damage.

Diode D1 prevents any damage occurring if the battery is connected the wrong way round. Capacitor C3 'decouples' the circuit from the supply, to maintain a steady voltage for the IC.

Breadboard construction (Figure 3.15)

Note that C3 and D1 are not required in this temporary layout.

1 Fit the IC the correct way round.
2 Fit the wire links and one or two demonstration presets.
3 Fit the other components, checking that C2 is the correct way round.

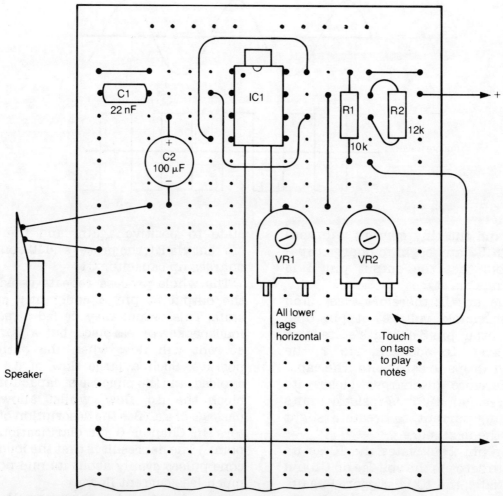

Figure 3.15 Electronic organ: layout diagram for breadboard construction
(Note: There are 5 wire links, plus the link which should be touched against the preset tags. Only 2 demonstration 'notes' are included. D1 and C3 are not included.)

4 Fit the wire which is used to touch the left bottom pin of the presets to play a note.
5 Fit the speaker leads and power supply leads.

Stripboard construction (Figure 3.16)

1 Begin by labelling the board as usual with the tracks running left to right. Mark the positions of the breaks.
2 Break the tracks as indicated.
3 Solder in the IC holder, wire links and resistors, noting that R2 must stand upright, with one lead bent around its body.
4 Solder in the diode and capacitors, noting that D1, C2 and C3 must be fitted the correct way round.

5 Connect the battery clip the correct way round, and a pair of wires to the loud-speaker and the 'keyboard'.
6 Fit the 555 timer IC making sure it is the correct way round.
7 Construct the keyboard.

Keyboard
The 'keyboard' may be constructed in a variety of ways, and the following is just a suggestion. Select a piece of wood long enough to house the number of 'notes' required. Cut some strips of aluminium foil (or any other similar conductive material), about the same width as a piano note. Some constructors may wish to shape the strips to create the same arrangement as a piano layout – including the 'black notes'.

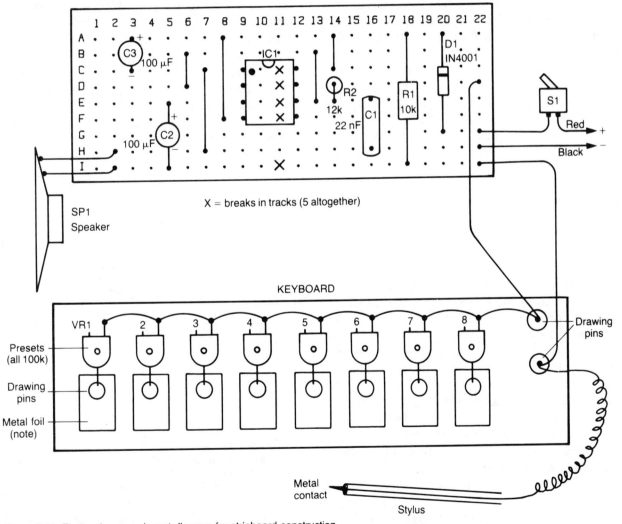

Figure 3.16 Electronic organ: layout diagram for stripboard construction
(Note: There are 5 wire links.)

The strips of foil should be fixed to the wood with glue or double-sided sellotape. Drawing pins may be fixed at the ends of the foil to act as an anchor for the presets. A preset may now be soldered to each drawing pin, as shown in Figure 3.16. This may well prove more difficult than it sounds, and it is essential to place a film of solder over each drawing pin *before* attempting to join the preset. If the solder appears reluctant to coat the drawing pin, place the soldering iron firmly against the pin for some time. Remember that solder will not form a bond until the temperature of the metal being soldered reaches the melting point of the solder. Filing or rubbing the pin with sandpaper may help.

If the drawing pins refuse to be soldered, as may happen with a low-power soldering iron, wind some bare wire around the underside of each pin and solder the preset to that.

Use wire to connect one of the other leads on each preset, as shown. The stylus may be made from an old pen. First remove the centre part, leaving only the plastic case. Push a piece of wire (stiff wire if possible) down through the case and shape the end so that it is secure as shown. Fasten the other end to the wooden base. Finally connect the 'keyboard' to the organ circuit.

Testing

Connect the supply, switch on and touch the 'stylus' (or wire) against a 'note'. On the breadboard construction a 'note' is one of the bottom pins of a preset. A sound should be heard from the loudspeaker. If nothing happens, try another 'note'. If the circuit still fails, switch off and check for faults.

If all is well, the organ must now be 'tuned' – if possible, with the aid of another musical instrument. Each preset must be adjusted to provide the exact note required. The preset values indicated will provide a fairly wide range of notes, but the entire pitch may be increased by reducing the value of C1. For example, halving the value of 0.01 μF will roughly double the frequency produced. Conversely, doubling the value of C1 to 0.047 μF (nearest value) will roughly halve the frequency.

The NE555 timer IC is remarkably stable, and even if the battery voltage changes a little, the notes produced should not. However, an additional preset resistor could be included in series with the preset resistor chain if overall frequency control is required. A value of about 10 kΩ will provide enough control to keep the instrument tuned. It should be mounted on the wooden base, and connected in series with one of the wires linking the circuit with the 'keyboard'. Adjust this preset to a position about midway, *before* tuning the organ.

Reducing the volume

If the organ proves to be a little too loud, the volume may be reduced by connecting a resistor in series with the speaker (Figure 3.17). In other words, disconnect one of the speaker wires (or cut it), and connect the resistor in such a way that the electricity must flow through the resistor on its way to the speaker. The value of the resistor required may be found by trial and error, but as a guide, a 1 kΩ resistor will substantially reduce the volume. Alternatively, a variable resistor or preset may be employed if desired.

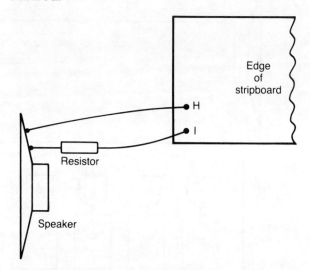

Figure 3.17 Diagram to show how a resistor may be connected in series with the speaker for the purpose of (a) raising the total impedance in the speaker circuit to more than 50 Ω, if a speaker of less than 50 Ω is used, and/or (b) reducing the volume of sound produced by the speaker.

Fault finding

(Read the section on 'Fault finding' in Chapter 6.)

If the organ refuses to work even after the usual visual checks, begin by checking that the IC, diode, electrolytic capacitors and supply connections are the correct way round.

Use a voltmeter to check the voltage from pin 8 (+) to pin 1 (−) of the IC. A reading just below the supply voltage should be registered. Move the positive lead of the voltmeter to pin 4 of the IC. The same reading should be obtained. If either of these tests fail, check the diode carefully, and the positive and negative connections to the IC.

Now place the positive voltmeter lead on the tip of the 'stylus'. Several volts should be registered if R1 and the stylus connections are wired correctly.

Beyond this, fault finding is difficult without additional equipment, and a very thorough check of the remaining components is recommended.

CMOS 555 IC

A CMOS version of the 555 timer IC may be used in this circuit, but, unlike the timing circuit described previously, the saving in current consumption will be slight.

741 Light or Temperature Sensor

Suitable supply voltage: 6 to 12 V d.c. In practice the IC will almost certainly work on 5 V, but this is not guaranteed.

Applications

Light sensor: automatic room lights, car parking light, automatic curtains, burglar alarm etc.

Temperature sensor: thermostat, fridge or freezer breakdown alarm, ice warning, fire alarm etc.

In this project, the voltage at one of the inputs to the IC is controlled by the resistance of a light dependent resistor (LDR) or a thermistor. The LDR has been discussed in Chapter 2 (light activated switch). The use of the IC provides more sensitivity and control. A thermistor is a temperature-sensitive device: as the temperature changes the resistance of the thermistor changes. Various types of thermistor are available; the one suggested here is a miniature bead thermistor of about 5 kΩ at room temperature. However, other types could be experimented with.

Components

Semiconductors
IC1   741 op-amp (8 pin DIL)
Tr1   transistor BC184L
D1   diode 1N4148 (required only if a relay is used)
D2   diode 1N4001 (not BB)
L1   LED, about 10.mA, (optional)

Resistors (any type) (for 9 to 12 V operation)
R1   5.6 kΩ (green, blue, red, 'any')
R2   1.5 kΩ (brown, green, red, 'any')
R3   1.5 kΩ
R4   47 kΩ (yellow, violet, orange, 'any')
R5   4.7 kΩ (yellow, violet, red, 'any')
R6   1 kΩ (brown, black, red, 'any')
      or 2.2 kΩ (red, red, red, 'any') on 5 V supply

R7   1 kΩ (required if LED is used)
      or 220 Ω (red, red, brown, 'any') on 5 V supply
VR1   preset, min. horizontal, 10 kΩ.
light dependent resistor (LDR) type ORP12 and/or thermistor (miniature bead) about 4.7 kΩ at 25°C.

Capacitors
C1   100 µF electrolytic, 16 V or more (not BB)

Miscellaneous
stripboard (0.1 in pitch) 7 cm by 3.5 cm (not BB) (at least 26 holes by 11 tracks)
IC socket, 8 pin DIL (not BB)
relay (see guide in Chapter 1)
battery connector and battery (optional)
insulated connecting wire
bare wire (tinned copper) for links (24 SWG approx.)

The 741 operational amplifier (OP-AMP)

The 741 is a cheap and popular linear integrated circuit. Like the NE555V it may be used in countless applications and whole books have been written about the 741 alone. It is available from many manufacturers and will normally be purchased in an 8 pin dual-in-line (DIL) package, like the NE555V. It may also be found in other packages, such as the 14 pin DIL, or TO-5 circular metal encapsulation. If you have problems operating the 741 on a 5 V supply, another IC, type 3140, is available, which may be used in place of the 741. It may be more expensive, but is designed for supplies down to 4 V.

The 741 is often used with 'dual power supplies'. In other words, a supply consisting of positive, zero and negative outputs. In this circuit, however, a 'normal' supply is employed.

How it works

The 741 is an amplifier with a very high gain. In other words, a very small change in voltage at its inputs causes a very much greater change at its output. The two inputs

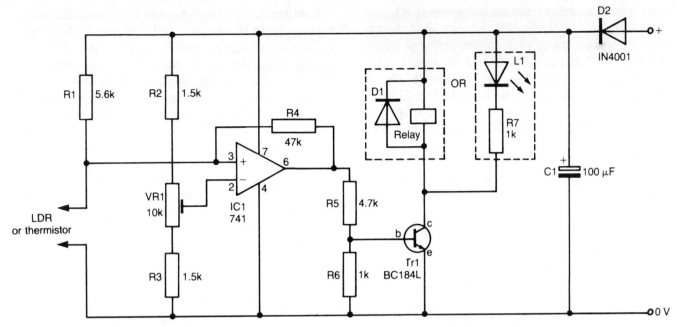

Figure 3.18 741 light or temperature sensor: circuit diagram. The output is connected to a relay (and protective diode), or LED (and series resistor), or both. For lower voltage operation, R6 = 2.2k and R7 = 220 Ω.

are denoted 'non inverting' (+) and 'inverting' (−). When set up correctly, a rise in voltage at the non inverting input (pin 3) will cause a much greater *rise* at the output (pin 6). A rise in voltage at the inverting input (pin 2) will cause a much greater *fall* in voltage at the output.

As illustrated in the circuit diagram (Figure 3.18), pin 7 of the IC is connected to positive, and pin 4 to 'zero'. Since the voltage at the inputs to the IC must be able to rise *and* fall, they must be held at approximately half the supply voltage. The inverting input is fed from the resistor chain R2, VR1 and R3. With VR1 set to about mid-way, the voltage at pin 2 should be about half the supply.

The voltage at pin 3 will be half the supply voltage if the LDR (or thermistor) has the same resistance as R1. With both inputs at half the supply voltage, in theory, the output will be at about half the supply voltage as well. In practice this may not be the case as the output will tend to swing towards zero or positive. This type of circuit is known as a **comparitor** where the two input voltages are compared. If the voltage at pin 3 is higher than that at pin 2, the output will go positive. If the voltage at pin 2 is higher than

that at pin 3, the output will go negative (or fall to zero in this case).

The situation may be likened to a seesaw, where the two inputs are the people at each end and the position of the seesaw is the output. It is quite difficult to make it balance exactly halfway — it tends to swing down on one side or the other.

In this circuit, VR1 is set to make the output voltage just fall to near zero. As the light *decreases* on the LDR, its resistance *rises* causing the voltage at pin 3 to *rise*. Eventually, this will 'tip the balance' and cause the output at pin 6 to swing towards the supply voltage. The result will be similar if the LDR is replaced with a thermistor. As the thermistor *cools*, its resistance *rises*. This is summarised as follows.

LDR
As light *decreases*, resistance *rises*, output from 741 goes *high*.
As light *increases*, resistance *falls*, output from 741 goes *low*.

Thermistor
As temperature *decreases*, resistance *rises*, output goes *high*.
As temperature *increases*, resistance *falls*, output goes *low*.

The opposite effect can be achieved if R1 and the LDR (or thermistor) are swapped. In all cases the setting of VR1 controls the point at which the output changeover occurs.

Resistor R4 provides 'positive feedback'. If the output voltage is near zero, this will tend to hold down the voltage at pin 3 slightly, until the resistance of the LDR (or thermistor) has risen so much that the output at pin 6 has to rise. As it does so, the rising voltage, via R4, reinforces the voltage at pin 3. The effect is that the output voltage swings very rapidly from near zero to near positive. If the resistance of the LDR (or thermistor) now decreases, R4 will tend to hold pin 3 positive until the decrease in resistance is so large that the output voltage has to fall. The change is again reinforced by R4 and the output swings very rapidly to near zero.

To sum up, R4 ensures that the output from the IC is either 'high' or 'low'. There will be no uncertainty as the light or temperature decreases. The output will swing 'high' and then remain 'high' even if the light or temperature then increases slightly. This effect is known as **hysteresis** and is essential in some applications. For example, if the circuit is used to sense darkness and make some curtains draw automatically, it would not be helpful if the curtains closed then

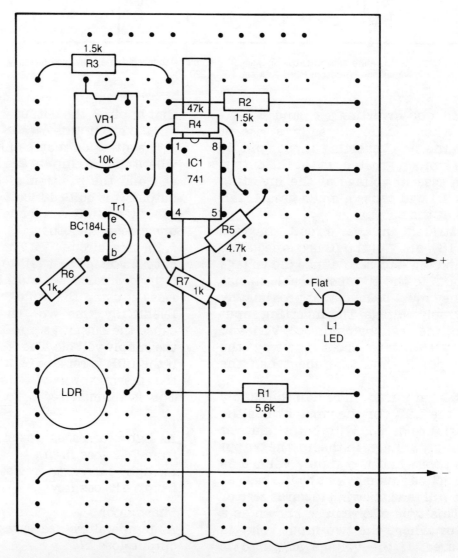

Figure 3.19 741 light or temperature sensor: layout diagram for breadboard construction
(Note: There are 3 wire links.
     For temperature sensing, replace the LDR with a thermistor. C1, D1 and D2 are not included.)

opened several times as passing clouds varied the light intensity at the changeover point.

Without R4 there will still be some hysteresis, and the circuit will appear more sensitive to changes in light or temperature. Even greater sensitivity may be obtained if R4 is connected from pin 6 to pin 2. Now the feedback will be *negative*, and it will be possible to make the voltage at pin 6 equal to about half the supply voltage by careful adjustment of VR1. The circuit will now be very sensitive to slight changes in light or temperature.

The output from pin 6 is fed into the base of transistor Tr1 via the potential divider comprising R5 and R6. This is to ensure that when the output from pin 6 is 'low', the voltage at the base is less than 0.6.V and the transistor is turned completely off. When the output from pin 6 goes 'high', the voltage at the base of Tr1 will be at least 0.6.V and the transistor will turn on. With Tr1 turned on, the relay and/or LED will operate. Diode D1 is to prevent back e.m.f. from the relay damaging the transistor, and R7 limits the flow of current through the LED.

Capacitor C1 decouples the supply and diode D2 prevents damage if the supply is connected with the wrong polarity.

Breadboard construction (Figure 3.19)

Note that the diagram shows the LED and R7, not the relay and D1. A relay may be fitted if required, providing it will operate on the supply voltage chosen and has a coil resistance of at least $100\,\Omega$ (6 V type) or $150\,\Omega$ (12 V type). Diode D2 and capacitor C1 are not included.

1 Fit the IC the correct way round.
2 Fit the preset, carefully bending the right hand pin underneath so that it fits in the correct line of holes.
3 Fit the wire links, then the other components, checking that the transistor and LED are the correct way round. A LDR is shown in the diagram. This may be substituted with a thermistor if required.

Stripboard construction (Figure 3.20)

Note that D1 may be omitted if a relay is not required.

1 Label the stripboard.
2 Solder in the IC socket and break the tracks between the pins, not forgetting the break in hole A7.
3 Solder in VR1, the wire links and then the other components, ensuring that the diodes, transistor and C1 are the correct way round.
4 If a LED is required, resistor R7 should be soldered in series with one of its leads as shown. Ensure that the LED is connected the correct way round.
5 Solder in the wires to the relay coil and/or LED and R7. A light dependent resistor or thermistor may be connected directly to the stripboard, or via longer wires.

Alternatives

The circuit turns *on* as the resistance of the LDR or thermistor rises. If you require the opposite effect, move the flexible wire from stripboard hole I1 to hole B1, and solder resistor R1 from holes F2 to I2. In other words, exchange R1 with the LDR/thermistor.

For greater sensitivity, remove resistor R4, or, for negative feedback (see 'How it works'), connect R4 from hole C10 to E10.

Testing

Connect the power supply and turn preset VR1 to make the LED or relay switch on and off. If all is well, set VR1 so that the LED/relay is just off. Now shade the LDR. The LED/relay should switch on. If using a thermistor, set VR1 so that the LED/relay is just on. Now warm up the thermistor by holding it in your fingers. After a few seconds the LED/relay should turn off.

Fault finding

(Read the section on 'Fault finding' in Chapter 6.)

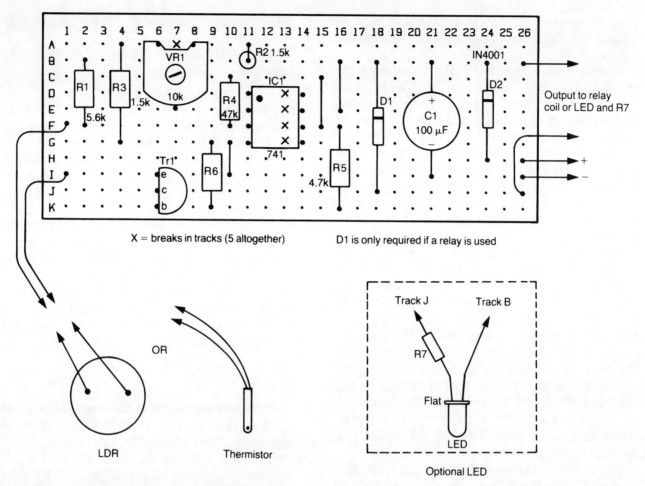

X = breaks in tracks (5 altogether)   D1 is only required if a relay is used

LDR   OR   Thermistor

Optional LED

Figure 3.20 741 light or temperature sensor: layout diagram for stripboard construction
(Note: There are 3 wire links.)

If the LED/relay will not turn on at all, disconnect the LDR/thermistor. If it still fails to work check that pin 6 of the IC is within a volt or so of the supply voltage. If it is, the fault lies around Tr1. If not, then IC1 or nearby components are at fault. The voltage at pin 2 should be at about half the supply voltage (after adjusting VR1). The voltage at pin 3 should be nearly equal to the supply (with the LDR/thermistor removed).

If the LED/relay remains on at all settings of VR1, join the two LDR connections together so that pin 3 of the IC is connected to zero volts. The LED/relay should now turn off. If it does, then the LDR or thermistor may have a resistance outside the range allowed for. It may be possible to correct this by raising (or lowering) the value of R1 to match. Experiment with different values. If the LED remained on, check the voltages as described in the previous paragraph, noting that the voltage on pins 3 and 6 of the IC should be within a volt or so of zero (with the LDR connections joined together).

Pre-amplifier

Suitable supply voltage: 6 to 16 V d.c. In practice, the IC will almost certainly work on 5 V, but this is not guaranteed.

Application

Microphone amplifier: Most microphones and record decks with magnetic pick-ups provide a very low-level output signal. For example, a moving coil microphone may provide less than 1 mV. This is too little for 'power amplifiers' and a pre-amplifier (pre-amp) must be employed between the microphone and power amplifier. The circuit to be described is intended for use with moving coil microphones. Other devices may be used, such as magnetic record decks, but no frequency correction network (required to extract the best quality from magnetic record decks) is included in this design.

The 741 op-amp is used in this design, and although specialised pre-amp ICs provide the best quality, very acceptable results may be obtained with this circuit.

Components

Semiconductors
IC1 Op-amp type 741 (8 pin DIL)

Resistors (in each case, the fourth band should be gold, red or brown)
R1 100 kΩ (brown, black, yellow)
R2 100 kΩ
R3 56 kΩ (green, blue, orange)
R4 1 kΩ (brown, black, red)

Capacitors (all 25 V or more)
C1 0.22 μF (any type)
C2 100 pF polystyrene (not BB)
C3 10 μF electrolytic
C4 10 μF electrolytic
C5 100 μF electrolytic (not BB)

Miscellaneous
IC socket, 8 pin DIL (not BB)
stripboard, 0.1 in pitch, about 8 cm by 3 cm (not BB) (at least 29 holes by 8 tracks)
socket suitable for the moving coil microphone employed, or the record deck output
small metal case (not BB)
screened cable
insulated connecting wire
bare wire (tinned copper) for links (24 SWG approx.)

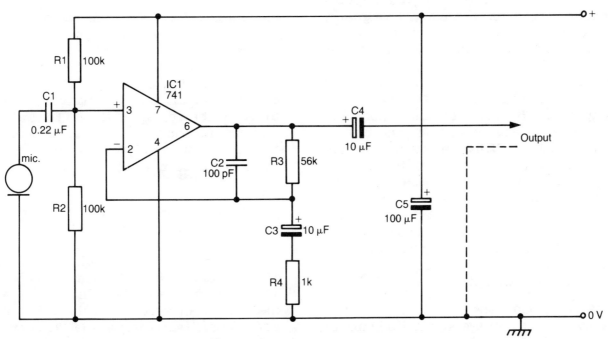

Figure 3.21 Pre-amplifier: circuit diagram

How it works

The gain of op-amp ICs tends to be very high. The gain of the 741 is typically 200 000 at zero frequency. In other words a change of signal at the input will cause a signal change 200 000 times larger at the output. In practice, such an enormous gain would cause many problems, and it can be reduced by feeding part of the output back into the inverting input of the IC. This is known as 'negative feedback'. Thus, as the input at pin 3 rises the output also rises, but since part of the output is fed to inverting input pin 2, the actual signal from pin 6 will be somewhat less. The actual gain of the IC can therefore be set by careful choice of the resistor in the 'feedback loop'.

Dual or single power supply

The 741 is often used with 'dual power supplies'. Pin 7 should be connected to positive, pin 4 to negative, with a 'zero volts' line acting as 'ground'. Thus the inputs and output from the IC can be kept at an average of zero volts, and can rise above zero or fall below zero when handling an alternating audio signal.

As this project employs a single supply, the inputs and outputs must be held at about half the supply voltage — to avoid clipping the tops or bottoms of an a.c. audio signal. A pair of resistors may be used to hold the input voltage at around half the supply voltage, and capacitors prevent any flow of d.c. from the junction between the resistors or from the output pin 6 to ground.

Capacitor C5 decouples the supply and provides a steady voltage for the circuit. Resistors R1 and R2 form a potential divider, maintaining a voltage equal to half the supply, at pin 3. The alternating signal produced when you speak into the microphone passes via capacitor C1. C1 prevents d.c. flowing from the junction between R1 and R2 to ground. The signal at pin 3 is amplified by the IC, the amplified signal appearing at output pin 6.

Negative d.c. feedback

Ideally, the d.c. voltage at pin 3 should be equal to half the supply voltage, and the d.c. level at pin 6 should also remain at half the supply voltage. However, the high gain of the IC will tend to cause the d.c. output at pin 6 to rise to the supply voltage or fall to zero, thus removing the top or bottom half of any a.c. signal present. Clearly this would be unacceptable.

Thus resistor R3 is used to connect the output to the inverting input pin 2. Any d.c. voltage change at the output will now cancel itself out, since it will be inverted by the IC. The capacitors C3 and C2 will have no effect since they cannot conduct d.c.

The circuit therefore has unity d.c. gain. In other words, the d.c. level at the input equals the d.c. level at the output, i.e. about half the supply voltage in each case.

Partial negative a.c. feedback

With resistor R3 alone, there would also be unity a.c. gain and the IC would not amplify at all. We therefore need to prevent most of the a.c. signal at output pin 6 feeding back to inverting pin 2. This is the purpose of capacitor C3. Capacitors appear to conduct a.c., and the larger the capacitor, the lower the frequency they will easily conduct. C3 conducts virtually all audible a.c. frequencies so that none are available at the inverting input.

The a.c. gain of the amplifier would be much higher than required, leading to problems of instability — uncontrollable oscillation resulting in a high pitch whistle at the output. Resistor R4 thus reduces the flow of a.c. through the capacitor, allowing sufficient to remain at the inverting input pin 2 to reduce the a.c. gain of the IC. In effect, the resistors R3 and R4 form a potential divider for a.c. signals. (Potential dividers are explained in Chapter 6, page 00.)

Specification

For those who like figures, the approximate audio signal **gain** of the amplifier is given by $(R3/R4)+1$. In this circuit the gain is therefore 56 k divided by 1 k, plus 1, in other words a gain of 57 times (or about 35 dB). The input impedance (see Chapter 6 for the meaning of impedance) is the value of R1 and R2 as if wired in parallel. This gives a value of 50 kΩ.

Capacitor C2 removes very high unwanted frequencies from the output. Capacitor C4 is necessary as the d.c. voltage at pin 6 is at about half the supply voltage. The capacitor therefore blocks the flow of direct current from pin 6, whilst allowing the a.c. audio signal to pass.

Breadboard construction (Figure 3.22)

1 Fit the IC the correct way round.
2 Fit the links and other components, ensuring that C3 and C4 are the correct way round. (C2 and C5 are unlikely to be required.)

Although screened cables are recommended in permanent circuits, ordinary connecting leads may be satisfactory in this type of construction. Their use will not stop the circuit working – but you may pick up hum and other unwanted signals.

Stripboard construction (Figure 3.23)

1 Label the stripboard.
2 Make the required breaks in the tracks, and solder in the IC socket.
3 Solder in the wire links and components, ensuring that the electrolytic capacitors are fitted the correct way round.
4 It is essential to use **screened cable** for the inputs and outputs, otherwise the circuit will pick up hum and other interference.
5 Complete the power supply connections and plug in the 741 IC the correct way round.

Testing

Connect the input to a microphone or record deck via a suitable plug/socket if necessary. If the microphone is fitted with a din plug (a circular plug of about 1.5 cm in diameter,

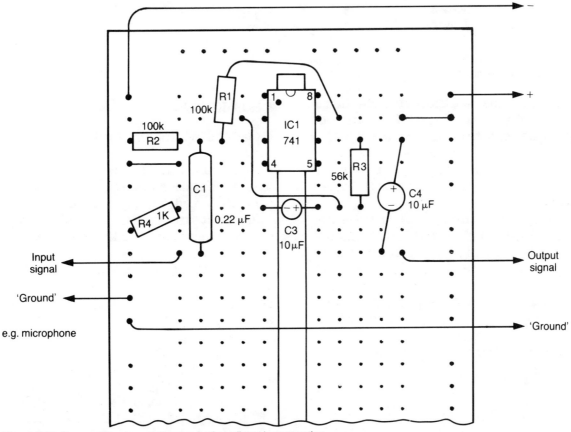

Figure 3.22 Pre-amplifier: layout diagram for breadboard construction
(Note: There are 3 wire links. C2 and C5 not required.)

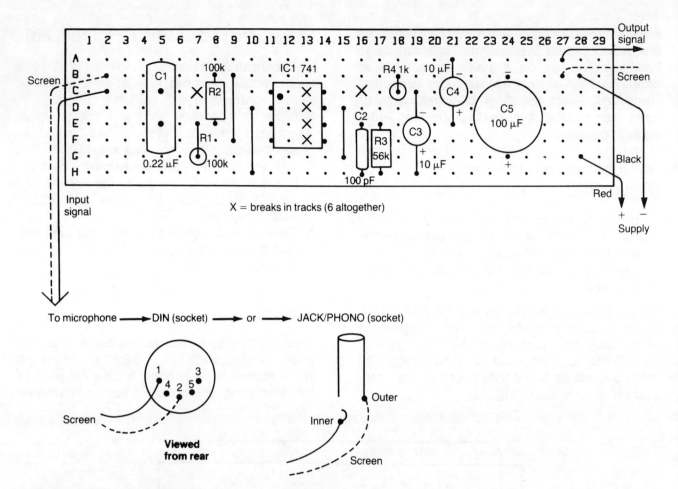

Figure 3.23 Pre-amplifier: layout diagram for stripboard construction
(Note: There are 3 wire links.)

with 3 or 5 pins inside), the signal should be present at pin 1, with pin 2 acting as 'ground'. Otherwise try pin 3 for the signal — or open up the microphone's din plug to check its wiring! Connect the pre-amp's output to a power amplifier or high impedance earpiece.

Connect a power supply to the pre-amp, and check that it amplifies with little distortion and little hum. In practice, the circuit is very sensitive to outside interference and should therefore be housed in a *metal* case with the case connected to 'ground' or zero volts on the pre-amp. *Ensure that the tracks and wires on the stripboard do not touch the metal case or a short-circuit will occur.*

Fault finding

(Read the section on 'Fault finding' in Chapter 6.)

Check the voltage across pins 7 (positive) and 4 (negative) of the IC. The voltage at pins 2, 3 and 6 should be about half this figure, but this may be difficult to measure unless a very good quality meter is available with a high resistance.

If the circuit still fails to work, a thorough visual check should locate the fault. An oscilloscope, if available, will verify if a signal is present at pin 3 and output pin 6.

Power Amplifier

Suitable supply voltage: 9 V d.c. For maximum power, a supply of up to 20 V may be used. This allows the amplifier to produce an output of nearly 3 W.

Applications

Headphone amplifier, speaker amplifier, computer amplifier, intercom, etc.

This amplifier is based on an integrated circuit type LM380. It may be used to amplify the audio signals from crystal or ceramic record player pick-ups, crystal microphones, tape decks or any similar source. It will not work well with very low-level sources, such as moving coil microphones or magnetic pick-ups, unless a pre-amplifier is also used.

The circuit is designed for a speaker (or headphones) with an impedance of 8 Ω. (See page 118 for the meaning of 'impedance'.) Speakers or headphones with a higher impedance may be used, but the sound level possible will be lower.

Components

Semiconductors
IC1 audio amplifier type LM380
D1   diode 1N4001 (not BB)

Resistors
VR1 potentiometer (pot), 25 kΩ, log.
     (for BB, use a 22 kΩ or 25 kΩ preset
     (min. horizontal)

Capacitors (all 25 V or more)
C1 4.7 µF electrolytic
C2 470 µF electrolytic
C3 1000 µF electrolytic

Miscellaneous
IC socket, 14 pin DIL (not BB)
stripboard (0.1 in pitch) about 8 cm by 3 cm
  (not BB) (at least 28 holes by 8 tracks)
knob for VR1 (not BB)
PP3 battery clip (optional)
screened cable for input and VR1
  (Screened cable consists of an inner insulated wire, surrounded by a wire 'screen'. The screen prevents electrical interference reaching the inner wire.)
speaker: 8 Ω impedance (or higher)
on/off switch (any type)†
insulated connecting wire
bare wire (tinned copper) for wire links (24 SWG approx.)

How it works

The heart of the circuit, the LM380 IC, is best viewed like a 'black box' which receives a small audio signal at pin 2, and provides a

† Potentiometers can be bought with on/off switches included

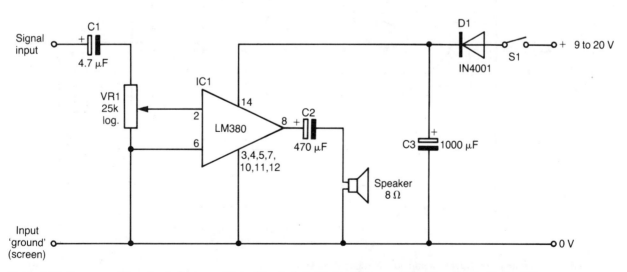

Figure 3.24 Power amplifier: circuit diagram   (Note: Pins 3, 4, 5, 10, 11, 12 are connected together inside the IC.)

much amplified (enlarged) signal at pin 8. Pins 3, 4, 5, 6, 10, 11 and 12 are connected to the negative or zero line, and pin 14 is connected to positive. (Note that pins 3, 4, 5, 10, 11 and 12 are connected together inside the IC.)

Diode D1 prevents damage to the circuit if the power supply is accidentally reversed. Capacitor C3 is a decoupling capacitor which ensures that a very steady voltage level is maintained across the IC.

Capacitor C1 allows the a.c. audio signal to pass, but prevents any flow of d.c. The audio signal then passes through the potentiometer VR1. The centre connection of VR1 is able to sweep from zero to full power, controlling the signal level fed into pin 2. Thus VR1 is a volume control. A log. (logar-

ithmic) type should be used if possible; it will provide a much more even response than a lin. (linear) type, since our hearing responds to sound on a logarithmic scale. (Note that log. presets are not normally available.)

The amplified a.c. audio signal appears at pin 8 of the IC. Unfortunately a d.c. source is also present, and this would cause problems for the loudspeaker if allowed to flow. Capacitor C2 thus blocks the flow of d.c., but allows the a.c. signal to flow.

Breadboard construction (Figure 3.25)

1 Fit the IC the correct way round.
2 Bend the left-hand pin of VR1 so that it

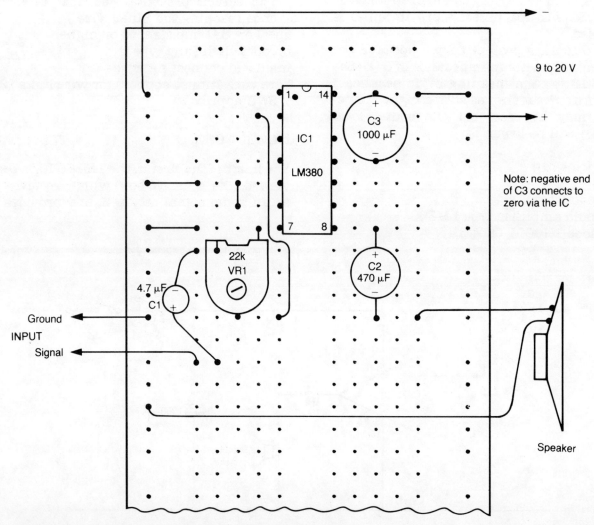

Figure 3.25 Power amplifier: layout diagram for breadboard construction
(Note: There are 5 wire links. D1 is not required. VR1 is a preset (not a standard potentiometer).)

fits the correct line of holes as shown. (A standard potentiometer may be used if preferred, in which case it must be joined with wires to the three preset connecting points.)

3 Fit the links and other components, ensuring that all three capacitors are the correct way round. (Note that D1 is not included.) Ordinary connecting wires may be used for the input, although screened cable is recommended in permanent circuits.

Stripboard construction (Figure 3.26)

1 Label the stripboard
2 Make the required breaks in the tracks, and solder in the IC holder.
3 Solder in the wire links.
4 Fit and solder the diode and electrolytic capacitors the correct way round.
5 Connect the loudspeaker wires and power supply wires.

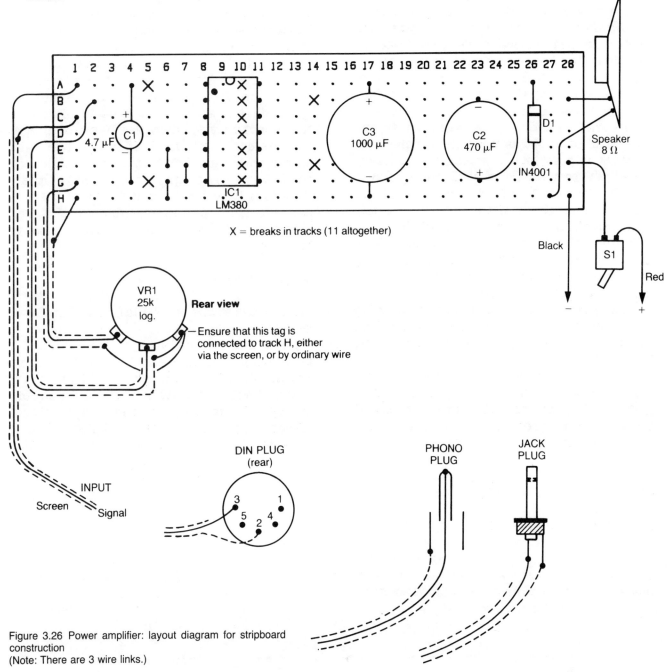

Figure 3.26 Power amplifier: layout diagram for stripboard construction
(Note: There are 3 wire links.)

6 VR1 may be connected with ordinary wires, but for best results use screened cable as shown.

7 Connect screened cable to the input.

8 Fit the IC into its socket the correct way round.

Testing

Check the stripboard carefully for mistakes and bridged tracks. Amplifiers are susceptible to a problem, where the output signal finds its way back to the input – and is re-amplified. This is known as **positive feedback** and causes a very unpleasant whistle (often heard when microphones are used too near loudspeakers). Positive feedback can occur in this type of circuit when an output lead is too close to an input lead. To prevent this, ensure that the wires are neat, and as short as possible. (If positive feedback is a serious problem, try connecting a $2.7\,\Omega$ resistor on track G, near pin 8 of the IC. Connect a $0.1\,\mu F$ capacitor to the other side of the resistor, and solder the other lead of the capacitor to track H.)

Connect the power supply and turn VR1 fully clockwise (or fully anticlockwise if you have wired it back to front – a common mistake!). Wet your fingers and touch the 'signal input' wire. A faint hum or crackle should be heard from the loudspeaker. The amplifier may also be tested by connecting the signal input to the speaker output of the electronic organ circuit described earlier. Alternatively, use any other speaker output (e.g. a battery-driven radio). Speaker output signals will not provide a good quality signal for the amplifier, and should only be used for testing.

Connecting up the amplifier

For higher quality, use the line output from a tape recorder, or 'monitor' output from a hi-fi system, or the output from the pre-amp described previously. Alternatively, the earpiece jack output from a small tape recorder, radio or computer may be used.

Types of connector

If phono connectors are employed on the tape recorder etc., the centre pin will carry the signal, and the outer metal should be connected to 'ground' (i.e. the screen of the cable). Some types of equipment (e.g. small computers) use 3.5 mm jack connectors. In this case the tip of the jack plug carries the signal, with the rest of the metal connected to 'ground'. Din connectors are very common and present the greatest problems since there are numerous types – and numerous pins in each! Attempts have been made to standardise the din connector system, but there are plenty of exceptions. In general you should find 5 pins arranged as shown in Figure 3.26. They are numbered rather oddly. Pin 2 (the centre pin) is always 'ground' (the screen of the cable). Pin 3 is the most likely to carry the signal. If this is not the case, try pin 1. If the output is in stereo, then pins 3 and 5 will probably carry the left and right signals respectively. Otherwise it will be pins 1 and 4. If you wish to connect this mono amplifier to a stereo signal, simply join the left and right outputs together.

Fault finding

(Read the section on 'Fault finding' in Chapter 6.)

Since most of the work is done by the IC, fault finding is limited. Use a voltmeter to check the voltage from pin 14 (+) to pin 7 (−) of the IC. It should be at about the supply voltage. Try feeding the audio input signal direct to pin 2 of the IC. This will test whether the fault is in the area of C1 or VR1.

4 PROJECTS USING LOGIC INTEGRATED CIRCUITS

Logic circuits are described in more detail in Chapter 6, but for those wishing to begin constructing immediately, the following points should be read carefully.

There are a number of types of logic ICs. The following circuits employ the '74HC' and '74LS' types. The 74HC series comprise CMOS (pronounced see-mos) ICs. The 74LS series comprise TTL ICs. All these terms are explained in Chapter 6, but for now remember the two types used are:

74HC (CMOS) and 74LS (TTL)

74HC (CMOS)

Of these two types, the 74HC (CMOS) is much better in most respects. It may be used in all the circuits in this chapter and uses very little current, making it ideal for battery-driven circuits. In fact, current consumption is so low that the IC may be left permanently connected to a battery without running it down for many months. The IC will operate on supplies of between 2 and 6.V. There is one problem however. It is easily damaged by static electricity. Once plugged into your circuit the other components will protect it from damage. The problem occurs as you remove the IC from its special package and try to plug it in. If your body is charged with static electricity, and you touch the pins, you may cause damage. The problem is not as bad as it sounds, providing you take simple precautions as follows.

Fitting CMOS integrated circuits
1 Keep the CMOS IC in its protective packaging until the moment of fitting in the circuit.
2 Touch an 'earthed' object *before* handling a CMOS IC. This may be a metal water pipe, or the metal case of an appliance connected to the mains supply — which may be switched on or off.

3 Try to touch the metal pins of the IC as little as possible when fitting into the socket.
4 Never leave any *input* to a CMOS gate unconnected. Unused inputs should be connected to the positive or 'zero' supply lines. In this chapter all the breadboard and stripboard layout diagrams include wire links to join unused inputs to 'zero'.

Breadboard circuits: Fit the ICs first, taking care to keep yourself 'earthed' (by touching an earthing point occasionally) while you fit the other components.

Stripboard circuits: Always use an IC socket — *never* solder in a CMOS IC directly. Fit the IC into the socket when the circuit is completely finished.

Despite the need for these precautions, the advantages of using CMOS ICs more than outweigh the precautions necessary.

74LS (TTL)

The 74LS (TTL) type can be freely handled without any precautions and may be a better choice in a classroom situation. It may be used in *some* of the circuits in this chapter in place of the CMOS IC. It requires exactly 5 V (no problem if you have built the 5 V regulator in Chapter 3), although in practice a new 4.5 V battery may work equally well. It uses far more current than a CMOS IC, making it less suitable for long-term battery use.

Which should you choose?

If you are building on stripboard and are prepared to be careful with the IC, choose the 74HC (CMOS) type. Even if you are using breadboard, the 74HC (CMOS) may still be used, but take even more care (for example, don't walk over a nylon carpet without 'earthing' yourself before you touch the circuit). If you have never handled an IC before, the 74LS (TTL) may be a better choice.

There are a large number of ICs of both types, and the one employed in many of the circuits in this chapter is the 74HC02 (CMOS) or 74LS02 (TTL).

When fitting an IC (of any type), check that it is the correct way round. You will find either a small indentation (dot) near pin 1 (the top left in all the layouts in this book), or a notch as shown in Chapter 1. Ignore any other dots which appear to be there to confuse you!

A decoupling capacitor is included in the circuit diagrams and stripboard layouts to enable the circuit to be used in a wide variety of situations. In the breadboard layouts the decoupling capacitor is very unlikely to be needed.

All the circuits may be powered from a 5 V d.c. supply. A 4.5 V battery may also be used, though it will have to be new to operate the 74LS (TTL) ICs properly.

WARNING: A 9 V supply will destroy these ICs.

Electronic Latch Switch

Suitable supply voltage: 4.5 to 5 V d.c.

Applications

Switching a light or other equipment on or off by pressing a push button switch or by touching your finger against a special contact.

The first project in this chapter shows how two logic gates may be connected to form a **bistable**. A bistable is a circuit which is able to remain in either of two states: for example, on or off. This may sound a complicated way of describing it, but the importance of the term 'bistable' will become clear when compared with the monostable and astable circuits described later.

The latch switch has two push button switches. When switch S1 is pressed, the circuit turns on, and remains on even when S1 is released. When S2 is pressed the circuit turns off, and then remains off until S1 is pressed again.

If the 74HC (CMOS) version of the IC is used, the push switches may be replaced with home-made touch contacts. In this case resistor R2 must be 10 MΩ.

Components

Semiconductors
IC1 integrated circuit type 74HC02 (or 74LS02)
Tr1 transistor BC184L
D1 diode 1N4001 or 1N4148 (required only if a relay is used)
L1 LED, about 10 mA, any colour)

Resistors (any type)
R1 1 kΩ (brown, black, red, 'any')
R2 1 kΩ
   or 10 MΩ (brown, black, blue, 'any') (see text)
R3 2.2 kΩ (red, red, red, 'any')
R4 220 Ω (red, red, brown, 'any')

Capacitors (16 V or more)
C1 0.01 μF any type
C2 100 μF electrolytic (not BB)

Miscellaneous
S1 push-to-make switch
S2 push-to-make switch
   (Note: S1 and S2 not required if touch contacts are used – see text)
stripboard (0.1 in pitch) 6 cm by 4 cm (not BB) (at least 22 holes by 12 tracks)
IC socket, 14 pin DIL (not BB)
insulated connecting wire

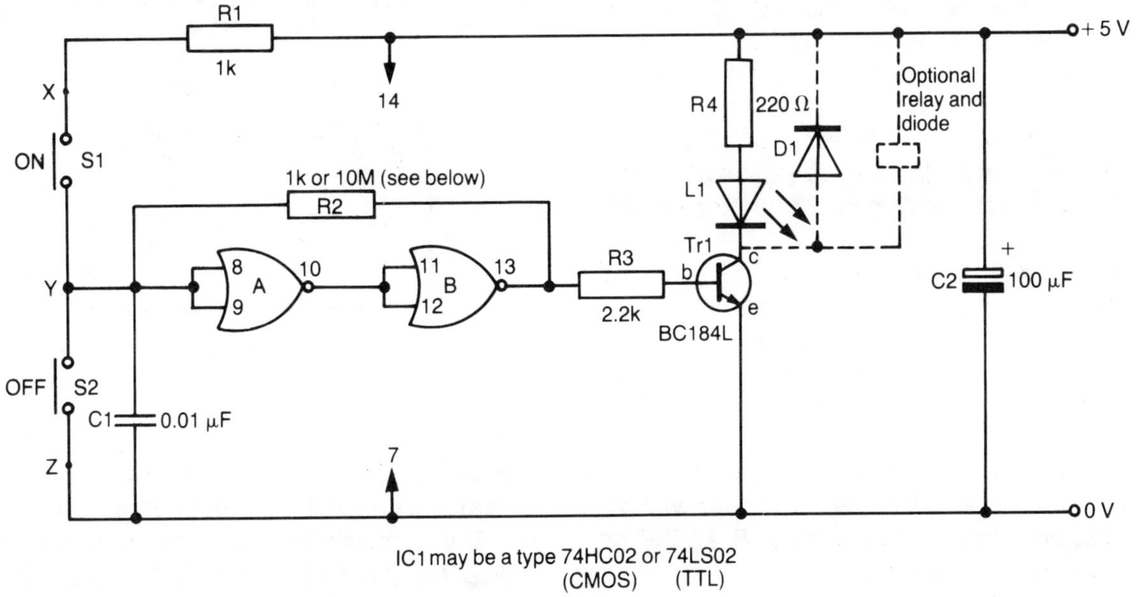

Figure 4.1 Electronic latch switch: circuit diagram
(Note: If IC1 is a type 74LS02, then R2 must be 1 kΩ, and S1, S2 must be push switches. The same circuit will also work with type 74HC02. If 'touch contacts' are required in place of S1 and S2, then IC1 must be a type 74HC02 and R2 must be more than 1 MΩ (10M is suggested).

bare wire (tinned copper) for wire links (24 SWG approx.)

How it works

Two logic NOT gates are required in this circuit (Figure 4.1). A number of ICs would satisfy this requirement, but the one chosen (mainly because it is one of the least expensive) is the type '02'. In other words, 74HC02 (CMOS) or 74LS02 (TTL). This IC contains four 2-input NOR gates. When their inputs are connected together, they behave as invertors or NOT gates. (See Chapter 6 for an explanation if necessary.)

As only two gates are required, the four spare inputs (two per gate) must be connected to positive or zero volts to prevent the spare gates oscillating or burning out.

When power is applied to the circuit the two input connections (pins 8 and 9) of gate A will be at zero volts. Gates A and B act as **invertors**. In other words, when both inputs are 'high' (nearly equal to the positive supply), the output is 'low' (nearly equal to zero volts). Thus, output pin 10 will be 'high'.

Since pin 10 is connected to the input pins 11 and 12 of gate B, with both B's inputs 'high' the output from pin 13 will be 'low'. It should be apparent then, that the output from pin 13 will be 'high' when pins 8 and 9 are 'high', and 'low' when 8 and 9 are 'low'.

Assuming that pins 8 and 9 are 'low' at present, when S1 is pressed the voltage applied to pins 8 and 9 will make gate A change state and its output go 'low'. With pins 11 and 12 'low', pin 13 will now go 'high'.

Current will now flow from pin 13 through resistor R2 to pins 8 and 9. Thus the output from pin 13 will hold the inputs at gate A 'high' even when S1 is released. Capacitor C1 conducts away any electrical noise which could cause the circuit to trigger accidentally. C1 also ensures that the circuit enters its 'off state' when power is first applied, since it holds pins 8 and 9 at zero volts for an instant.

With pin 13 'high', current will also flow via R3 (which limits it to a reasonable level) into the base of Tr1. This in turn switches on

Three drawing pins, screws or similar may be connected as follows:

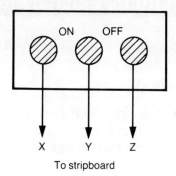

To stripboard

OR   Two sets of contacts may be wired as follows:

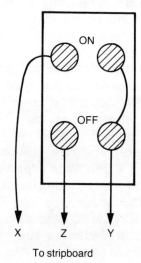

To stripboard

OR   Contacts may be made using bare wire, pushed through holes drilled near the corner of the plastic case:

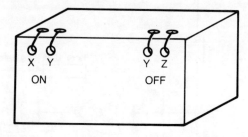

Figure 4.2 Touch contacts for electronic latch switch

Tr1, and current flows through the LED (L1) making it light. Resistor R4 limits the current through the LED to a safe level.

If you press S2, the voltage on pins 8 and 9 will fall to near zero. Thus pin 10 will go 'high', and this 'high' at pins 11 and 12 will cause pin 13 to go 'low'. This low output will hold the input to gate A 'low' via R2, even when S2 is released. With no current into its base, Tr1 will switch off, as will L1.

Resistor R1 prevents too much current flowing if S1 and S2 are pressed at the same time, and capacitor C2 decouples the supply, providing a steady voltage for the circuit.

Adding touch contacts

If you wish to use touch contacts instead of push switches, you *must* use the CMOS IC (74HC02), and R2 must be between 1 MΩ and 10 MΩ. The touch contacts may be home-made from drawing pins or even pieces of wire, as illustrated in Figure 4.2. When you touch the contacts a small electric current (too small to feel) will pass through your finger and operate the circuit. The touch contacts must be connected to points X, Y and Z on the circuit.

Breadboard construction (Figure 4.3)

Note that C2 is not required in a temporary circuit.

1 Take care to 'earth' yourself if using a CMOS IC.
2 Fit the IC the correct way round.
3 Fit the wire links – counting them carefully in case you forget one.
4 Fit the other components with Tr1 and L1 the correct way round.
5 Fit the wires and switches or touch contacts.

Stripboard construction (Figure 4.4)

WARNING: If the IC is a CMOS type it should be left safely in its protective packaging until required.

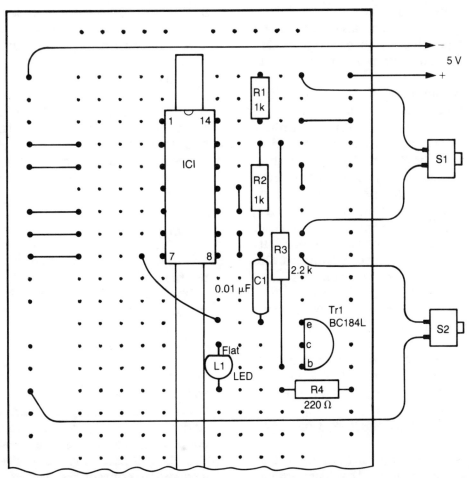

Figure 4.3 Electronic latch switch: layout diagram for breadboard construction
(Note: There are 10 wire links. C2 not included.)

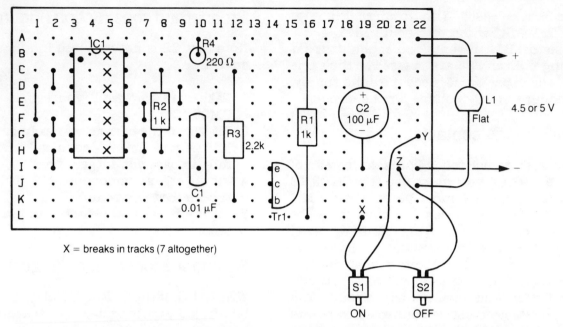

Figure 4.4 Electronic latch switch: layout diagram for stripboard construction
(Note: There are 8 wire links.)

1 Label the stripboard.
2 Position the IC holder and secure by bending (if possible) two of its pins flat against the copper strip at opposite corners.
3 Break the tracks between the pins of the IC holder, and solder it in place.
4 As stated above, the four unused inputs (pins 2, 3, 5 and 6) must be connected to positive or zero volts. In this circuit they are connected to zero. Several wire links are used and soldering these can be tedious. Use a long piece of bare wire, place through the first hole, solder, then pull it through the next hole *before* cutting it to size. This method enables the links to be fitted quickly, and should leave them straight and neat.
5 Solder in the resistors and capacitors, noting that C2 must be fitted the correct way round.
6 Fit the transistor the correct way round. Fit diode D1 from hole B17 to hole J17 with its band nearest the top, if a relay is to be connected.
7 Connect wires for the switches or touch contacts.
8 Connect wires for the LED (unless it is to be mounted directly to the stripboard) and power connections.

9 Fit the IC the correct way round. If a CMOS type, *take the precautions described at the beginning of this chapter.*

Testing

Connect the supply. The LED should not light. If it does, disconnect the supply and check for faults.

Press S1. The LED should light up and stay on. Now press S2. The LED should switch off and remain off.

Fault finding

(Read the section on 'Fault finding' in Chapter 6.)

Check that the correct breaks have been made in the tracks, and the IC, diode (if fitted), transistor and C2 are fitted the correct way round.

Now check the voltage across pin 14 (positive) and pin 7 (negative) of the IC. A reading of about 5 V should be obtained. If there is no reading, disconnect the battery and check carefully for short-circuits and correct power supply connections. Check that D1 (if fitted) is the correct way round and in the correct tracks.

If a reading is obtained, but the LED fails to

light at all, use a piece of bare wire to short across the emitter and collector of the transistor. If the LED still fails to light, the fault may lie around the LED or R4. Check that the LED is fitted the correct way round.

If the LED did light, use a spare resistor of between 1 kΩ and 10 kΩ to join the positive supply with the transistor base. If the LED now lights up, the fault lies in the area of gates A or B. Failure of the LED to light indicates the fault may be around the transistor.

Correct operation of gates A and B may be tested with a voltmeter. When the LED is off, the output from gate B should be 'low', and the output from gate A 'high'. When the LED is (or should be) on, the output from B should be 'high' and the output from A 'low'. Avoid measuring the voltage on the input pins to gate A, as many voltmeters will consume too much current to make the reading valid.

Connecting a relay

If you require a relay (see Chapter 1 for details), connect its coil to tracks B21 and J21 on the stripboard. Do not forget to add a protective diode as described earlier.

Doorbell Timer

Suitable supply voltage: 4.5 to 5 V d.c.

Other applications

Light switch timer (to allow light to remain on for a period of time after the switch is turned off), general purpose timer.

NOTE: Only the CMOS 74HC version of the IC may be used in this circuit.

This project illustrates how logic integrated circuit gates may be used as a **monostable**. A monostable is a circuit which may be triggered into an 'active' state, but then returns to its former state. In this case, when the doorbell push switch is pressed, a bell or buzzer sounds for a set period — regardless of the time for which the switch is pressed.

The circuit may be directly wired to a suitable sounding device, providing it consumes no more than 100 mA. Many modern bleepers and buzzers are well within this limit. Alternatively, the circuit will operate a relay, allowing it to drive any buzzer or bell.

Components

Semiconductors
IC1 integrated circuit type 74HC02
Tr1 transistor BC184L
D1 diode 1N4148 (may be omitted if a solid state buzzer or bleeper is used)

Resistors (any type)
R1 1 MΩ (brown, black, green, 'any')
R2 4.7 kΩ (yellow, violet, red, 'any')
R3 150 kΩ (brown, green, yellow, 'any')
R4 2.2 kΩ (red, red, red, 'any')

Capacitors 16 V or more
C1 0.22 μF any type
C2 0.01 μF any type
C3 22 μF electrolytic
C4 100 μF electrolytic (not BB)

Miscellaneous
S1 push button (push-to-make) switch
IC socket, 14 pin DIL (not BB)
stripboard (0.1 in pitch) about 7 cm by 3.5 cm (not BB) (at least 26 holes by 11 tracks)
sounding device, e.g. buzzer or bleeper
insulated connecting wire
bare wire (tinned copper) for wire links (24 SWG approx.)

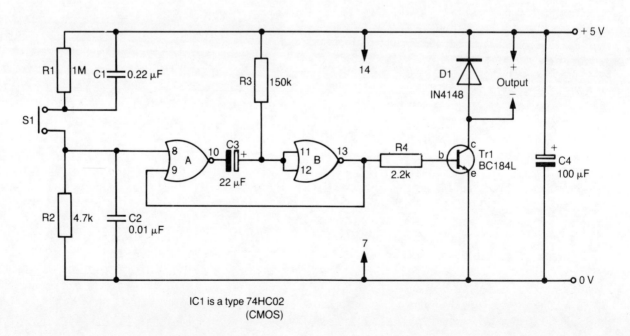

Figure 4.5 Door bell timer: circuit diagram

How it works

Two NOR gates are required for this circuit. A NOR gate produces a 'high' (nearly the supply voltage) output if *neither* of its inputs is 'high'. If either or both inputs goes 'high', the output goes 'low' (nearly zero volts).

It is not possible to purchase just two NOR gates. The IC specified has four gates, two of which are therefore not used.

The circuit (Figure 4.5) is arranged so that an input to gate A switches on gate B. This in turn feeds back into A thus holding the circuit 'active'. This active state is temporary, and the circuit returns to its 'standby' mode when capacitor C3 is charged. The time taken for C3 to charge determines the time for which the circuit is 'active'.

A CMOS IC uses so little current that it may be permanently connected to a battery. To trigger the circuit a positive pulse is required at input pin 8 of gate A. There are several ways of achieving this, but for reliable results a network comprising R1, R2, C1 and C2 is employed.

On standby, resistor R2 holds the voltage into pin 8 at zero. Since long wires may be used between the circuit and push switch S1, there is a strong possibility of interference (for example, mains hum) being picked up and falsely triggering the circuit. Thus capacitor C2 is used to 'short out' any a.c. interference.

Triggering the circuit

During 'standby', R1 will ensure that the voltage both sides of C1 is 'high' (i.e. supply voltage). Note that with both sides of C1 at the same voltage, we say that it is **discharged**. If S1 is pressed, this 'high' will connect with pin 8, triggering the circuit. After a fraction of a second C1 will be fully charged (i.e. the end connected to S1 will have fallen to nearly zero volts), as R2 is much lower in value than R1. When S1 is released, current flowing through R1 now discharges C1 (i.e. both sides are now 'high').

This rather complicated arrangement is designed to eliminate switch contact bounce. Most switches — especially the types used on front doors — do not switch 'cleanly'. In other words, as they switch on or off their contacts vibrate, sending several pulses to a circuit. In simple arrangements this is of no importance, but in this circuit such contact bounce may cause the IC to re-trigger as the switch is released.

Monostable

During standby, both inputs to gate A will be 'low'. Thus, output pin 10 will be 'high' (see Chapter 6 for clarification if necessary). Resistor R3 will ensure that the other side of capacitor C3 is also 'high'. With pins 11 and 12 'high', gate B's output will be 'low'. Thus transistor Tr1 will be switched off.

When a 'high' pulse is received at input pin 8, output pin 10 becomes low. This negative output pulse passes via C3 in the same way as an alternating current. Thus pins 11 and 12 become 'low', and output pin 13 goes 'high'. This 'high' feeds back into pin 9 thus holding output pin 10 'low', and ensuring that the circuit remains 'active' even after pin 8 has returned to zero volts. All this happens in the fraction of a second for which the 'high' pulse was received at pin 8.

With the output from gate B 'high', current flows via limiting resistor R4 into the base of transistor Tr1. The transistor is therefore turned on and current flows from positive through the sounding device or relay and through the transistor to zero. Diode D1 shorts out any high voltages produced by some sounding devices or relays.

At present, both sides of capacitor C3 are at about zero volts. Thus there is a potential difference (a difference in voltage) across resistor R3. Current therefore flows from positive through R3 and begins to charge capacitor C3. The voltage at pins 11 and 12 now rises as C3 charges, and eventually it is high enough to 'trigger' gate B and reduce its output to zero. The transistor therefore turns off.

Input pin 9 also returns to zero volts, and with both inputs to gate A at zero, pin 10 becomes 'high'. With both sides of capacitor C3 'high', the circuit has returned to its original standby mode.

Capacitor C4 decouples the supply, providing a steady voltage for the circuit.

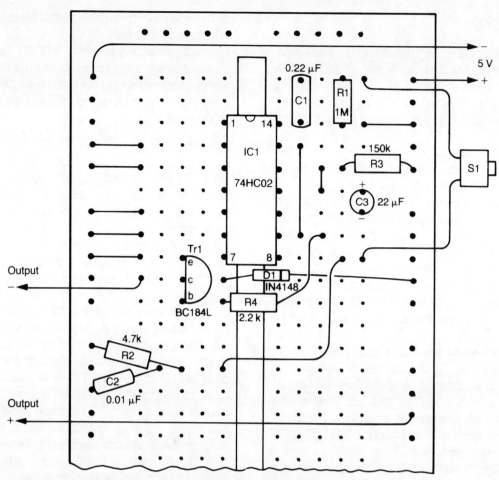

Figure 4.6 Door bell timer: layout diagram for breadboard construction
(Note: There are 9 wire links. IC1 must be type 74HC02. C4 is not included.)

Breadboard construction (Figure 4.6)

Note that C4 is not required in a temporary circuit.

1 'Earth' your fingers before handling the CMOS IC.
2 Fit the IC the correct way round.
3 Fit the wire links – counting them carefully in case you forget one.
4 Fit the other components with Tr1, D1 and C3 the correct way round. D1 is not required if a solid state (or transistorised) buzzer or bleeper is used.
5 Fit the other wires and switch.

Stripboard construction (Figure 4.7)

WARNING: The IC is a CMOS type and should be left safely in its protective packaging until required.

1 Label the stripboard.
2 Position the IC holder and secure by bending (if possible) two of its pins flat against the copper strip at opposite corners.
3 Break the tracks between the pins of the IC holder, and solder it in place.
4 Solder in the wire links, resistors and capacitors, noting that C3 and C4 must be fitted the correct way round. Even though two of the gates in IC1 are not required, their input pins *must* be 'tied' to zero as shown to prevent the gates oscillating and/or burning out.
5 Fit the transistor and diode the correct way round. Note that fitting diode D1 the wrong way round may destroy the transistor.
6 Connect wires as indicated.
7 Fit the CMOS IC the correct way round,

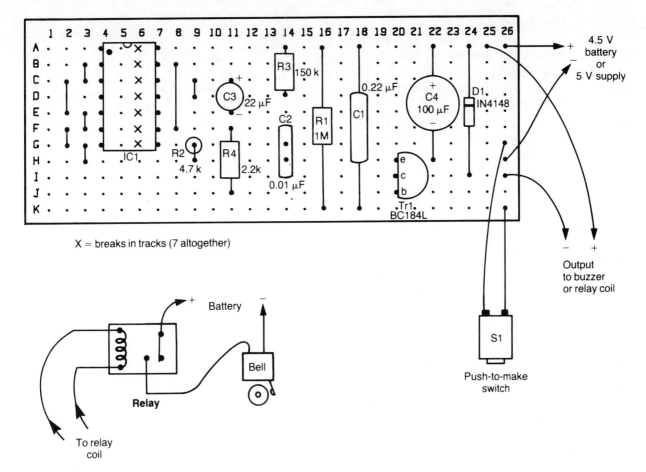

X = breaks in tracks (7 altogether)

Figure 4.7 Door bell timer: layout diagram for stripboard construction
(Note: There are 7 wire links.)

taking the precautions described at the beginning of this chapter.

Testing

Connect the power supply. Press S1 and check that the circuit switches on for a short time, then switches off. The length of time for which S1 is pressed should not affect the result in any way.

Fault finding

(Read the section on 'Fault finding' in Chapter 6.)

If the circuit fails to work, begin by checking the voltage supply from pin 14 (+) to pin 7 (−).

Next, check the voltage at output pin 13. When triggered, it should rise to nearly the supply voltage. If it does, then the fault lies around Tr1 or the sounding device or relay.

If the output at pin 13 remains 'low', check the voltage at pin 10. On standby it should be nearly equal to the supply. Using a small piece of wire, carefully join pin 8 to the positive supply. The voltage at pin 10 should fall to zero. If it does not, gate A or its associated wiring are seriously at fault.

If the last test caused the circuit to work normally, the fault may lie in the area of R1, C1 or possibly R2 or C2.

When checking voltages around a CMOS IC, note that the current used by the voltmeter can upset some parts of the circuit. You will not cause any damage, but false readings may be obtained. For example, you may not be able to measure the voltage at pins 11 and 12, as the current used by the voltmeter may discharge the capacitor C3.

Changing the time period

The length of time during which the circuit is 'active' after pressing S1 depends upon the values of R3 and C3. If either R3 or C3 is doubled in value, the time period will double. Similarly the time period may be halved by halving either R3 or C3. Some constructors may prefer to calculate their own combination of values. The approximate time period in seconds is given by the capacitance of C3 (in farads) multiplied by the resistance of R3 (in ohms). To avoid awkward numbers, the formula may be rewritten as follows:

approximate time in seconds =
$$R3 \text{ (in } M\Omega) \times C3 \text{ (in } \mu F)$$

If the value of C3 is 22 μF and R3 is 150 kΩ (= 0.15 MΩ), the time will be approximately:

$$22 \text{ (}\mu F) \times 0.15 \text{ (}M\Omega) = 3.3 \text{ seconds}$$

If variable times are required, a potentiometer or preset could be used for R3. Note that different capacitors of the same value may give different time periods as the value of an electrolytic capacitor is not particularly accurate.

Heads and Tails Indicator

Suitable supply voltage: 4.5 to 5 V d.c.

This circuit simulates the tossing of a coin. When the push button switch is pressed, a light (LED) flashes on and off at a high rate. When the button is released the light may be on, or off, and now remains in that state. The light on represents a head, and off represents a tail.

Two of the CMOS gates are now wired to form an **astable** circuit. Such a circuit oscillates or switches on and off repeatedly.

Components

Semiconductors
IC1 integrated circuit type 74HC02 (or 74LS02) (Note that the 74HC02 IC will produce a better balance between heads and tails)
Tr1 transistor BC184L
L1 LED, about 10 mA, any colour

Resistors (any type)
R1 1 kΩ (brown, black, red, 'any')
R2 1 kΩ
R3 4.7 kΩ (yellow, violet, red, 'any')
R4 220 Ω (red, red, brown, 'any')

Capacitors (any type)
C1 0.1 μF
C2 0.1 μF (not BB)

Miscellaneous
S1 push-to-make switch
stripboard (0.1 in pitch) about 7 cm by 4 cm (not BB) (at least 25 holes by 12 tracks)
IC socket, 14 pin DIL (not BB)
insulated connecting wire
bare wire (tinned copper) for wire links (24 SWG approx.)

How it works

Figure 4.8 shows the circuit diagram. Gates A and B of the IC are wired to form an astable multivibrator or **oscillator**. In other words, they rapidly switch on and off. When push button switch S1 is pressed, the 'oscillator' circuit is connected to gate C, which in turn feeds gate D. These gates thus switch on and off with the oscillator. When S1 is released, gates C and D remain in whatever state they happened to be last in. The output from gate D drives a LED via transistor Tr1.

In more detail
When power is first applied to the circuit, the inputs to gates A and B will be 'low' (off). Thus both outputs from A and B will start to

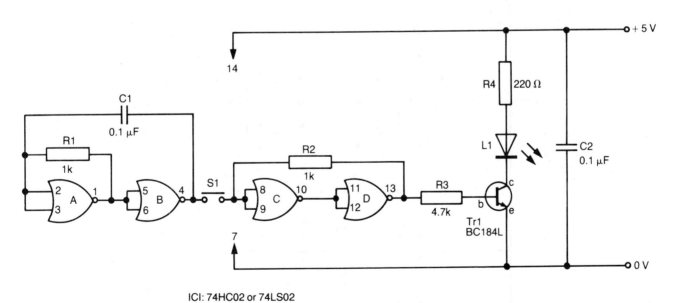

ICI: 74HC02 or 74LS02
(CMOS)   (TTL)

Figure 4.8 Heads and tails indicator: circuit diagram

rise in voltage. In practice, one gate will always rise faster than the other. We will assume that gate A switches on first.

With the output from pin 1 'high', pins 5 and 6 will also be 'high' and the output from gate B will be 'low'. The capacitor C1 will now begin to charge from the 'high' output of gate A, via resistor R1. The time taken will depend upon the values of R1 and C1, and is a fraction of a second with the values indicated.

After this time the voltage across C1, and therefore the voltage at pins 2 and 3, will be enough to trigger gate A, resulting in its output going 'low'. With pins 5 and 6 now 'low', gate B's output will go 'high'. A positive pulse will now appear to flow through C1 (like a.c.), reinforcing the rising voltage at pins 2 and 3. This situation does not last long, since with output pin 1 now 'low' the voltage at pins 2 and 3 will fall as current drains into pin 1 via R1. The time taken depends again upon the values of R1 and C1.

After this time, the voltage at pins 2 and 3 will be sufficiently low to cause gate A's output to go 'high'. The chain of events now continues as before, with gates A and B both switching on and off alternately.

When S1 is pressed, the oscillating output from gate B is connected to the inputs of gate C. Gate C in turn feeds the inputs to gate D. Thus, if gate C's inputs are 'high' its output will be 'low', and with gate D's inputs 'low' its output will be 'high'. In other words, the output from gate D will be in phase (go on and off) with the inputs at gate C. If a CMOS IC is used, R1 may be increased to reduce the flashing rate of the LED. A value of $680\,\mathrm{k\Omega}$ produces quite a pleasing effect.

At the moment when S1 is released the output from gate B may be 'high' or 'low'. If it is 'low' the output from D will be 'low' and resistor R2 will ensure that the input pins 8 and 9 remain 'low'. If the output from gate B was 'high', gate D's output will be 'high', and R2 will hold the input pins 8 and 9 'high'. Thus gates C and D will remain in a fixed state, 'high' or 'low', depending upon the state of B at the moment S1 was released.

The output from gate D also feeds a

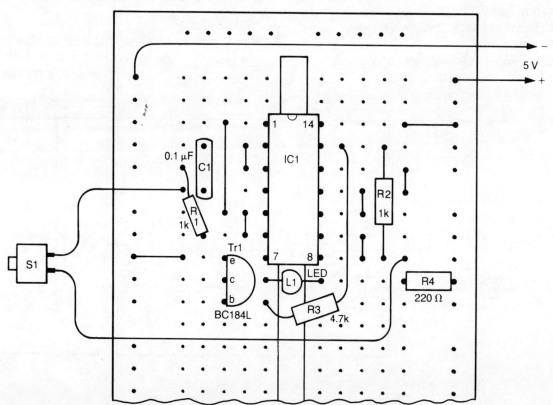

Figure 4.9 Heads and tails indicator: layout diagram for breadboard construction
(Note: There are 8 wire links. C2 is not included.)

transistor via current-limiting resistor R3. The transistor enables the small output current from gate D to operate the larger current required to drive the LED. Resistor R4 limits the current flowing through the LED, and capacitor C2 decouples the supply.

Breadboard construction (Figure 4.9)

Note that C2 is not required in a temporary circuit.

1 Take care to 'earth' yourself if using a CMOS IC.
2 Fit the IC the correct way round.
3 Fit the wire links — counting them carefully in case you forget one.
4 Fit the other components, taking care to fit Tr1 and L1 the correct way round.
5 Fit the wires for S1 and the supply. The bare ends of the wires may be either soldered to S1, or wound tightly round the tags and covered with tape.

Stripboard construction (Figure 4.10)

WARNING: If you use a CMOS IC, leave it safely in its protective packaging until required.

1 Label the stripboard.
2 Position the IC socket.
3 Break the tracks between the pins of the IC socket, and solder it in place.
4 Solder the wire links, resistors and capacitors.
5 Fit the transistor the correct way round.
6 Connect wires to the push-to-make switch S1.
7 Connect wires for the LED (unless it is to be mounted directly to the stripboard) and power connections.
8 Fit the IC the correct way round. If it is a CMOS type, take the precautions described at the beginning of this chapter.

Testing

1 Connect the supply and press switch S1. The LED should appear about 'half bright' since it is flashing too quickly to observe.
2 Release switch S1. The LED should remain on or off. Repeat this several times to check that the LED remains on or off in roughly equal proportions. The CMOS IC will achieve better results in this respect.

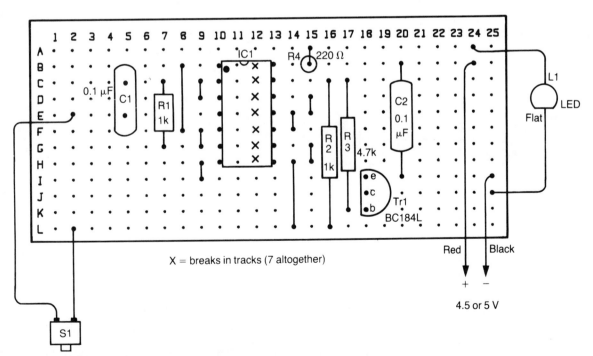

Figure 4.10 Heads and tails indicator: layout diagram for stripboard construction
(Note: There are 8 wire links.)

Fault finding

(Read the section on 'Fault finding' in Chapter 6.)

Begin by checking that there is no short circuit. Then check that the IC, transistor, and LED are fitted the correct way round. Check the supply across pins 14 (+) and 7 (−) of the IC.

If all is well, try connecting a 1 kΩ resistor from the positive supply to the base of Tr1. The LED should light. If it does not, the fault may lie in the region of the transistor.

If the last test worked, the fault may be in the area of one of the IC gates. Gates C and D may be checked by connecting the input pin 8 or 9 directly to the positive supply (in which case the LED should light), or directly to the negative (zero) supply (in which case the LED should not light). *During this test the switch S1 must not be pressed.* If this test fails, the fault lies in the links wired to gates C or D, or else in the oscillator circuit around gates A and B.

Quiz Game Indicator

Suitable supply voltage: 4.5 to 5 V d.c.

Applications

Various quiz games, snap, etc. Reaction tester.

This project enables two or more contestants to play any game where the first to answer gains a point. An obvious example is the card game 'snap'. Each contestant (or team) has a push button switch and a light. The first to press his button causes his light to switch on, and also prevents the opposing contestant's light working.

After each point is awarded, the 'master switch' is turned off to reset the circuit.

Components list

Semiconductors
IC1 integrated circuit type 74HC02 (or 74LS02)
Tr1 transistor BC184L
Tr2 transistor BC184L
L1 LED, about 10 mA, any colour
L2 LED, about 10 mA, any colour

Resistors (any type)
R1 1 kΩ (brown, black, red, 'any')
R2 1 kΩ
R3 4.7 kΩ (yellow, violet, red, 'any')
R4 4.7 kΩ
R5 220 Ω (red, red, brown, 'any')

Capacitors (any type)
C1 0.1 μF
C2 0.1 μF
C3 0.1 μF (not BB)

Miscellaneous
S1 push-to-make switch
S2 push-to-make switch
S3 on/off toggle switch, or push-to-break switch (see text) (not BB)
IC socket, 14 pin DIL (not BB)
stripboard (0.1 in pitch) about 7 cm by 4.5 cm (not BB) (at least 24 holes by 15 tracks)
insulated connecting wire
bare wire (tinned copper) for wire links (24 SWG approx.)

How it works

The circuit (Figure 4.11) divides into two halves. Push button 'S1' triggers gates P and Q, causing L1 to light up. These gates then 'latch' – in other words, the output is fed back into the input, causing them to remain triggered. The push switches are wired so that when either set of gates latches on, no power is available for the other push switch, and the other gates cannot be made to change state.

The IC contains four NOR gates. Each pair of inputs to the gates are joined together in this circuit. Thus each gate is simply being used as an **invertor**. In other words, a 'high' (voltage nearly equal to the positive supply) into any input, causes the output to go 'low' (voltage nearly equal to zero).

When power is applied to the circuit, capacitors C1 and C2 are not charged, so both sets of inputs to gates P and R are 'low' and their outputs are therefore 'high'. With one side of both switches S1 and S2 'high' they are both operational. The 'high' output from gate P causes gate Q to produce a 'low' output. Transistor Tr1 is therefore switched off, as is L1. By the same reasoning, L2 is also off.

If push switch S1 is pressed, the 'high' output from gate R will connect with the inputs to gate P. This 'high' input will cause the output from P to go 'low'. Hence push switch S2 will be made inoperative. This 'low' from P will cause gate Q's output to go 'high'. This is fed back to the inputs of gate P thus holding gates P and Q in this state. The 'high' output from Q is also fed via resistor R3 into the base of transistor Tr1, turning it on. With Tr1 turned on, current can flow via limiting resistor R5 and through L1, lighting it up. Thus, pressing push switch S1 has caused L1 to light and push switch S2 to become inoperative.

A similar sequence of events will occur if push switch S2 is pressed first, with L2 lighting and switch S1 becoming inoperative.

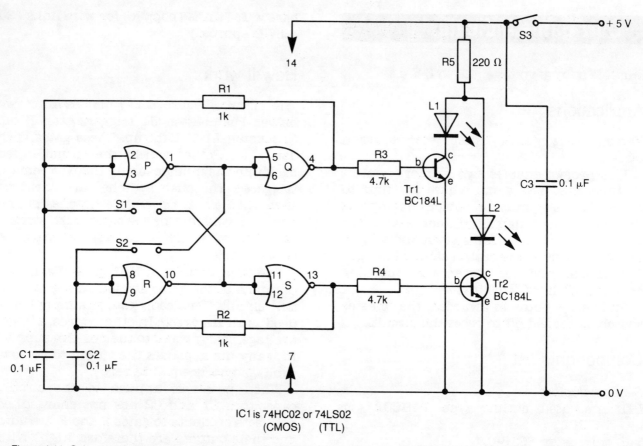

Figure 4.11 Quiz game indicator: circuit diagram

IC1 is 74HC02 or 74LS02
(CMOS)   (TTL)

Capacitors C1 and C2 increase the reliability of the circuit by ensuring that the inputs to gates P and R are held at zero volts, particularly at the moment when power is applied to the circuit. C3 decouples the supply.

Breadboard construction (Figure 4.12)

Note that S3 and C3 are not required in a temporary circuit.

1 Take care to 'earth' yourself if using a CMOS IC.
2 Fit the IC the correct way round.
3 Fit the wire links – counting them carefully in case you forget one.
4 Fit the other components, taking care to fit the transistors and LEDs the correct way round.
5 Fit wires for the switches and supply. The bare ends of the wires may either be

soldered to the tags on the switches or wound tightly round them and covered with tape.

Stripboard construction (Figure 4.13)

WARNING: If you are using a CMOS IC, leave it safely in its protective packaging until required.

1 Label the stripboard.
2 Position the IC holder and secure by bending (if possible) two of its pins flat against the copper strip at opposite corners.
3 Break the tracks between the pins of the IC holder, and solder it.
4 Solder in the wire links, resistors and capacitors.
5 Fit the transistors the correct way round.
6 Connect flexible wires to the push-to-make switches S1 and S2.
7 Connect the LEDs the correct way round

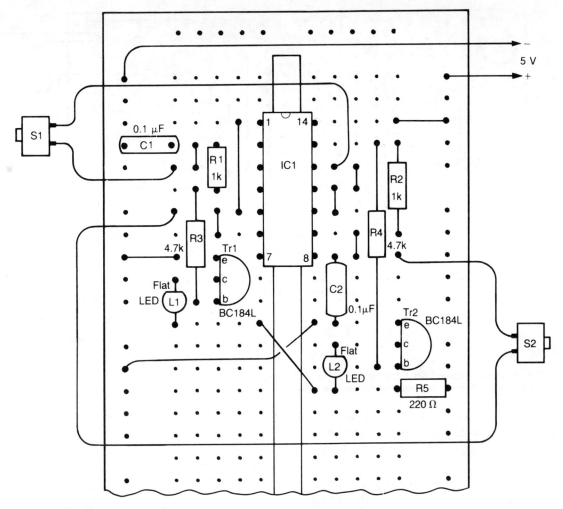

Figure 4.12 Quiz game indicator: layout diagram for breadboard construction
(Note: There are 10 wire links. S3 and C3 not included. Use insulated wire on push switches.)

via flexible wires and solder in the supply connections.

8 The main on/off switch should be connected in the positive lead as shown. This switch may be replaced with a push-to-break switch if preferred. A push-to-break switch is like a normal push button switch, except that it is normally on and switches off when pressed. In this type of circuit such a switch may be more convenient than a normal on/off type. A normal on/off switch may also be connected in series with the push-to-break switch. Alternatively, it may be left out, as the circuit uses very little power unless a LED is actually turned on.

9 Fit the IC the correct way round. If it is a CMOS type, take the precautions described at the beginning of this chapter.

Testing

1 Connect the power supply. Nothing should happen. If either LED lights, switch off and check for faults.
2 If all is well, press push switch S1. L1 should light up. Now press switch S2. L1 should remain lit and nothing else should happen.
3 Switch off S3, then switch on again; now try pressing switch S2. This time L2 should light and remain lit by itself even if S1 is pressed.

Fault finding

(Read the section on 'Fault finding' in Chapter 6.)

Begin by checking that there is no short-

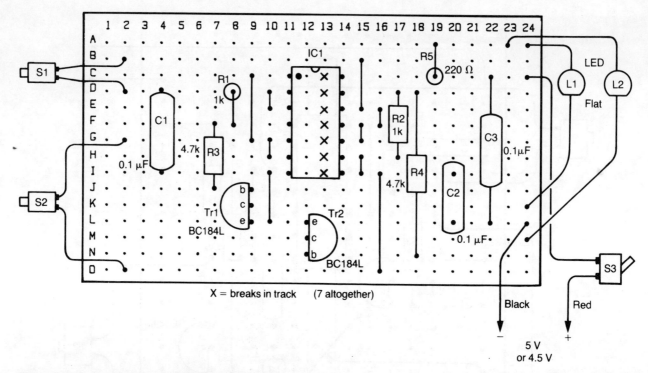

Figure 4.13 Quiz game indicator: layout diagram for stripboard construction
(Note: There are 9 wire links. R1 and R5 are mounted vertically.)

X = breaks in track   (7 altogether)

circuit. Then check that the IC, transistors, diode and LEDs are fitted the correct way round. Check the supply across pins 14 (+) and 7 (−) of the IC.

If neither (or just one) LED lights, use a small piece of bare wire to short together the emitter and collector leads of Tr1 or Tr2. In each case L1 or L2 should light. If they do not, then the fault may lie in the region of R5 or the LEDs.

If all is well so far, try connecting a 1 kΩ resistor from the positive supply to the base of Tr1 or Tr2. In each case L1 or L2 should light. If it does not, the fault may lie in the region of the transistors.

If the last test worked, the fault must be in the area of one of the IC gates. Connect the negative of the voltmeter to negative (zero) in the circuit. Now check that the readings on the various IC pins are as follows.

Pin	1	4	10	13
When power is applied	high	low	high	low
When S1 is pressed	low	high	high	low

(the next readings assume that power is switched off then on again)

When S2 is pressed	high	low	low	high

Note: 'high' means nearly equal to the positive supply voltage; 'low' means nearly equal to zero volts.

Reaction tester

The project may be used to compare the reaction speeds of two people. The 'Electronic timer' project (Chapter 3) could be fitted with a smaller timing capacitor to reduce the time delay and produce a starting signal.

Light Chaser Display

Suitable supply voltage: 4.5 to 5 V d.c.

Applications

Disco type lighting effects, Christmas tree lights, etc.; random number games.

This circuit will only work with 74HC (CMOS) ICs.

A chain of LED's is made to flash continually in sequence. The chasing speed may be varied by using a preset potentiometer. A simple modification will enable a light to be selected at random, and the project may therefore be useful for certain types of games.

Components list

Semiconductors
IC1   integrated circuit type 74HC02
IC2   integrated circuit type 74HC4017
L1—10 LED, about 10 mA, any colour (10 required) (less than 10 LEDs may be used if preferred)

Resistors (any type)
R1   10 kΩ (brown, black, orange, 'any')
R2   220 Ω (red, red, brown, 'any')
VR1   preset, min. horizontal, 1 MΩ

Capacitors (any type)
C1   0.1 µF
C2   0.1 µF (not BB)

Miscellaneous
IC socket, 14 pin DIL (not BB)
IC socket, 16 pin DIL (not BB)
stripboard (0.1 in pitch) about 8 cm by 5 cm (not BB) (at least 30 holes by 15 tracks)
insulated connecting wire
bare wire (tinned copper) (24 SWG approx.)

How it works

A new IC, type 74HC4017, is introduced in this circuit (Figure 4.14). This is a 'decade counter with completely decoded outputs'. In other words, it has ten outputs (plus a 'carry out'). When first switched on, output number zero (pin 3) is 'high', and the other outputs are 'low'. When a pulse is received at its clock input (pin 14), output 0 goes 'low', and output 1 (pin 2) goes 'high'. When the next

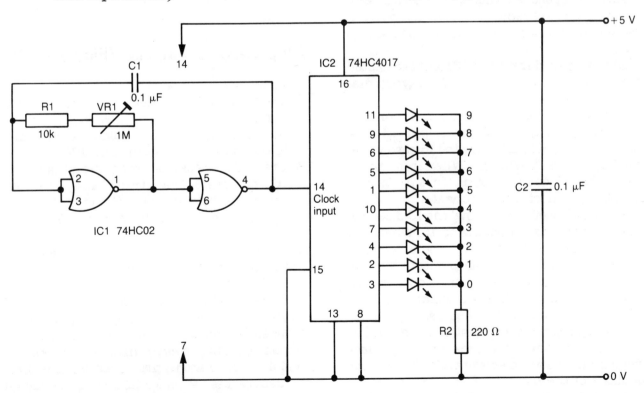

Figure 4.14 Light chaser display: circuit diagram

pulse is received, output 1 goes 'low' and output 2 (pin 4) goes 'high'.

This repeats in sequence until output 9 (pin 11) goes from 'high' to 'low', whereupon the IC resets and begins from output zero again.

Just to confuse you, the output numbers do not rise in sequence with the IC pin numbers. This is outlined in the circuit diagram, where pin 3 is output zero, pin 2 is output 1, pin 4 is output 2 etc.

The IC is able to supply enough current to drive a LED. The LEDs are connected to each output as shown. Resistor R2 limits the current flowing through each LED.

Pin 14 is called a 'clock input'. The term 'clock pulse' is often used in electronics and in this case a series of pulses ('highs') are fed to pin 14, causing the IC to count each time a pulse is received. In this circuit the pulses are generated by two gates of another IC, type 74HC02. The way in which this circuit operates is very similar to the first two gates of the 'Heads and tails indicator' and will not be described again. Preset VR1 allows the frequency to be changed, i.e. the number of pulses per second can be set to control the speed at which the LEDs cascade. Resistor R1 prevents a direct connection between output pin 1 and input pins 2 and 3 if VR1 is set to zero.

All the unused inputs of IC1 are connected to zero volts, as shown in the layout diagrams.

Returning to IC2, several other connections are provided as follows. pin 13 is a 'clock inhibit'. When connected to zero volts, the IC counts normally. When pin 13 is 'high', the IC cannot count. In this circuit pin 13 is connected to zero volts.

Pin 15 is 'reset'. When 'low' the IC does not reset except when it counts to 10. When pin 15 is made 'high' the IC resets to zero wherever it is. For example, if output pin 5 is connected to reset pin 15, the counter will reset each time it reaches a count of 6.

If pins 13 and 15 are not used for their intended purpose, they *must* be connected to zero volts or they will pick up stray electrical signals and interfere with the correct working of the IC.

Pin 12 is 'carry out'. This may be used to

drive the clock input pin of another similar IC to enable counting to 99.

Pin 16 is the positive supply connection, and pin 8 is the 'zero' supply.

Breadboard construction (Figure 4.15)

Note that C2 is not required in a temporary circuit. To simplify the arrangement, the line of holes normally used for the negative supply is used to connect the LED cathodes to R2.

1 Take care to 'earth' yourself, as both ICs are CMOS types.
2 Fit the preset VR1, taking care to bend the left-hand tag horizontal so that it does *not* make electrical contact.
3 Fit the ICs the correct way round, then the wire links. Insulated wire should be used for the long wire links. Count the number of links carefully to ensure that none have been forgotten.
4 Fit the other components, ensuring that the LEDs are the correct way round. Less than 10 LEDs may be used if preferred.
5 Fit the wires for the supply, noting the 'non standard' position of the negative lead.

Stripboard construction (Figure 4.16)

1 Label the stripboard.
2 Position the IC holders, noting that IC2 (on the left-hand side) is a 16 pin holder. Note also that the IC1 holder is fitted one track higher at the top than IC2.
3 Break the tracks between the pins of the IC holders. (The track may be left unbroken between pins 7 and 8 of IC1, in which case the link from tracks H to K in line 19 is not required.)
4 Solder in the IC holders and break the tracks at the other points indicated in the layout (7 extra breaks).
5 Solder the wire links and components. If you wish, outputs 9, 4 and 8 may be taken directly from the holes next to pins 11, 10 and 9 of IC2, to save three wire links.
6 Solder insulated wire links for the LED display. Less than 10 LEDs may be used if desired. The display may be arranged in

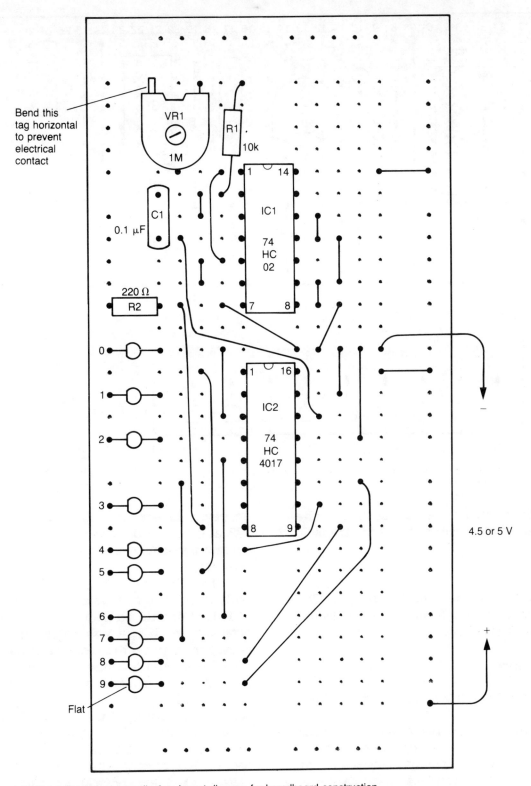

Bend this
tag horizontal
to prevent
electrical
contact

Flat

4.5 or 5 V

Figure 4.15 Light chaser display: layout diagram for breadboard construction
(Note: There are 21 wire links.
        C2 is not included.)

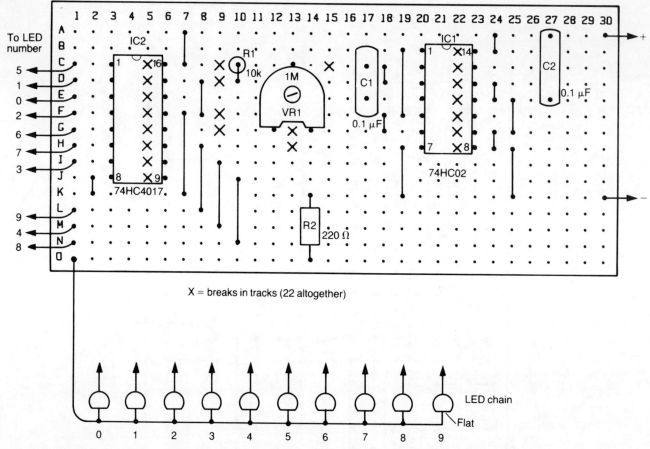

Figure 4.16 Light chaser display: layout diagram for stripboard construction (Note: There are 16 wire links.)

any convenient way, ensuring that all the cathodes ('flats') are connected to track O.

Testing

Connect a 4.5 V battery or 5 V supply. The LED display should light in sequence. Adjust VR1 for the best effect.

Fault finding

(Read the section on 'Fault finding' in Chapter 6.)

A common problem with this circuit is the LED display failing to light in the correct sequence. This is easily corrected by numbering the connections carefully according to the diagrams.

If no LED lights up, use a voltmeter to check the voltage across pins 16 and 8 of IC2. About 5 V should be obtained, otherwise the supply pins of the IC are not connected

properly. Check the connections between IC2 and the LEDs; check the LEDs are the correct way round, and their cathodes are all connected to R2.

If the LEDs fail to cascade, IC1 may be at fault. Check the voltage across pins 14 and 7 of IC1. It should be about 5 V. To check the output from IC1, a voltmeter may be connected from pin 4 to zero. A reading of about 2 to 3 V should be obtained, indicating that the output is probably oscillating correctly. If an oscilloscope is available, it may be connected instead of the voltmeter and will prove conclusively whether a train of pulses exists. If these tests fail, check the circuit around IC1 very carefully.

Repeat the test above at input pin 14 of IC2 to ensure that the pulses are reaching IC2. Check that pins 13 and 15 are connected to zero volts. Finally use a voltmeter to check the voltages at all the output pins of IC2.

Experiments and modifications

Some care must be taken when making modifications, as any CMOS input pin which is disconnected from the circuit could be damaged by static electricity. If possible, add the new links or components before disconnecting old ones.

The display may be 'frozen' using several methods, but probably the simplest is by 'shorting' capacitor C1. This prevents IC1 oscillating and thus IC2 cannot continue to count. A better method of inhibiting the count is to use 'clock inhibit' pin 13. Connect pin 13 to the positive supply via a resistor of between $10 \, k\Omega$ and $1 \, M\Omega$. Next remove the link joining pin 13 to zero volts. Make sure that pin 15 is still connected to zero, using a new link if necessary. Connect a push-to-make switch from pin 13 to zero volts. When the switch is pressed, pin 13 will be held at zero volts and counting will take place. When the switch is released, pin 13 will become positive and counting will stop.

To make IC2 reset to zero before it reaches 10, connect pin 15 to the appropriate output and disconnect the wire linking pin 15 to zero volts. For a 'dice indicator', only six LEDs are required, and output number 6 (pin 5) should be connected to reset pin 15.

Random Number Generator

Suitable supply voltage: 4.5 to 5 V d.c.

Applications

Board games, bingo and other games of chance; counter/timer, digital reaction timer.

This is a similar project to the last one, except that an illuminated number is displayed by a device known as a 'seven segment LED display'. These displays are often used in calculators, electronic timers and so on.

Note that IC1 may be a CMOS or TTL type, but IC2 must be CMOS.

Components list

Semiconductors
IC1 integrated circuit type 74HC02 (or 74LS02)
IC2 integrated circuit type 4026BE (the 'E' is not important)
seven segment 0.3 in common cathode LED display
Note: Details are also provided for a 0.5 in display which may be used if preferred.

Resistors (any type)
R1 1 kΩ (brown, black, red, 'any')
R2 10 kΩ (brown, black, orange, 'any') (or 1 MΩ if touch switch is required instead of S1)
R3 47 kΩ (yellow, violet, orange, 'any')

Capacitors (any type)
C1 0.1 μF
C2 0.1 μF (not BB)
C3 0.1 μF (optional – see text)

Miscellaneous
S1 push-to-make switch (a home-made pair of touch contacts may be used instead if preferred, providing R2 is 1 MΩ)
IC socket, 14 pin DIL (not BB)
IC socket, 16 pin DIL (not BB)
IC socket, 14 pin DIL for 0.3 in display (not BB)
stripboard (0.1 in pitch) about 8 cm by 3.5 cm (not BB) (at least 30 holes by 10 tracks)
insulated connecting wire
bare wire (tinned copper) (24 SWG approx.)

How it works

If you look closely at a seven segment LED display, you will see that the numbers are

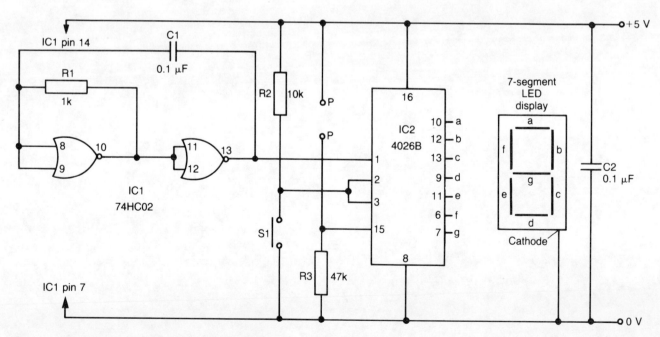

Figure 4.17 Random number generator: circuit diagram

produced by lighting up certain LED segments. Each of the seven segments is identified by a letter (see Figure 4.17). Thus to make a '1', segments b and c are illuminated; a '2' is produced by lighting up segments a, b, g, e and d, and so on. When all the segments light up together the number '8' is produced.

Making the appropriate segments light up for a given number is quite complicated and a number of ICs have been produced which will drive a seven segment display, automatically lighting up the correct segments. Most of these ICs require a number coded in binary. The IC used in this project is a counter and seven segment LED display driver combined. In other words, it is similar to the counter IC (74HC4017) used in the previous project, except that the outputs are able to drive a seven segment LED display directly. The IC is coded 4026BE and is one of the CMOS 4000 series. If an 'HC' version is produced at some future time, it is likely to be coded 74HC4026.

The 4026BE integrated circuit

Pin 1 is a 'clock input'. Each time a 'pulse' is received at pin 1, the count advances by 1.

Pin 2 is a 'clock inhibit'. When this is 'low' the counter works normally. When pin 2 is 'high' the IC will not respond to input pulses.

Pin 3 is 'display enable'. When 'high' the display is switched on, when 'low' the display is switched off, even though the IC will still count if required.

Pin 15 is 'reset'. When 'low' the IC only resets upon reaching a count of ten. If pin 15 is made 'high' the counter resets wherever it is.

Pins 6, 7, 9, 10, 11, 12 and 13 must be connected to the separate anodes of the seven segment LED display. The cathodes are internally connected together and must be connected to zero volts in the circuit. Thus it is essential to buy a **common cathode** display and not the 'common anode' type which is also available.

Various other pins are provided for special purposes, but the only one likely to be of interest is pin 5, 'carry out'. This provides a pulse every time the IC reaches a count of ten. If pin 5 is connected to the 'clock input' of another IC, the second IC will count in

tens. The second IC may be connected to another display, making a two-digit counter. In this case pins 2, 3 and 15 on the second IC must be joined to pins 2, 3 and 15 on the first, not forgetting the positive and zero supplies as well. Several ICs may be cascaded in this way, each driving its own display.

The 'clock pulse' for the IC is derived from IC1. This is similar to the method used in the previous project except that pins at the right of the IC are used, to aid the stripboard layout design. The way in which the circuit operates is similar to the first two gates of the 'Heads and tails indicator' and will not be described again.

When power is applied to the circuit, resistor R2 will cause pins 2 and 3 of IC2 to go 'high'. Thus the display will be on, but the IC will not be able to count, even though pulses are produced by IC1. When S1 is pressed, pins 2 and 3 will go 'low'. The display will now be 'disabled' (off), but the IC will start counting. When S1 is released the IC will stop counting again, and the display will light up. A very large number of pulses are received every second at pin 1, and therefore the number displayed when S1 is released is effectively random.

Resistor R3 ties the reset pin 15 to zero volts, to prevent IC2 resetting accidentally. Capacitor C2 decouples the circuit.

Breadboard construction (Figure 4.18)

Note that C2 is not required in a temporary circuit.

1 Take care to 'earth' yourself, as one or both ICs are CMOS types.
2 Fit the ICs and seven segment common cathode LED display. Insulated wire should be used for the long wire links. Count the number of links carefully to ensure that none have been forgotten.
3 Fit the other components and S1. If you require a touch switch, just fit wires for now.
4 Fit the wires for the supply.

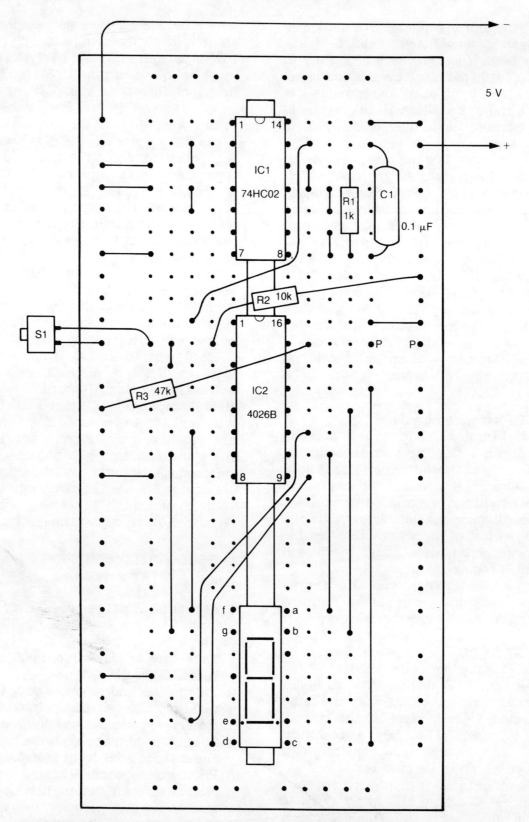

Figure 4.18 Random number generator: layout diagram for breadboard construction
(Note: There are 21 wire links.
       C2 is not included.)

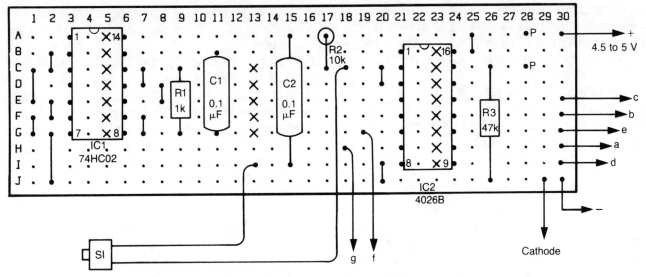

X = breaks in tracks (20 altogether)

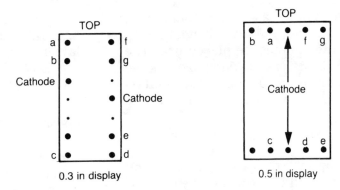

TOP

a   f
b   g
Cathode
  Cathode
  e
c   d

0.3 in display

TOP

b   a   f   g

Cathode

c   d   e

0.5 in display

Figure 4.19 Random number generator:
layout diagram for stripboard construction
(Note: There are 11 wire links.
    Common cathode display:
    only one cathode pin need be used.)

Viewed with pins towards you

COMMON CATHODE: Only one cathode pin need be used.

Stripboard construction (Figure 4.19)

1 Label the stripboard.
2 Position the IC holders noting that IC2 (on the right-hand side) is a 16 pin holder and is fitted one track below IC1 (at the top).
3 Break the tracks between the pins of the IC holders, plus five extra breaks as shown.
4 Solder in the IC holders.
5 Solder in the wire links (counting them carefully), followed by the components.
6 Solder insulated wire links for the common cathode display.
7 Fit the ICs the correct way round, taking the usual precautions.

Touch sensitive switch

In either layout, the push switch S1 may be replaced by a pair of touch contacts if preferred. This is possible because IC2 is a CMOS type and pins 2 and 3 require very little current. Thus R2 may be increased to 1 MΩ. If you now place your fingers over the bare ends of the wires which would have joined S1, enough current will flow through your skin to cause the voltage at pins 2 and 3 to fall to near zero. Your skin therefore acts like a switch. The project 'Electronic latch switch' described earlier in this chapter shows how touch contacts may be constructed.

If you use a 1 MΩ resistor for R2, a normal

push button switch will still work. The reason for indicating a value of 10 kΩ in the components list is to prevent erratic results if you accidentally touch the tags of S1.

Seven segment LED display

The display specified is a 0.3 in type. Other sizes are available, including the popular 0.5 in type. The 0.5 in display may be mounted sideways on the breadboard. However, it will not fit a standard 14 pin DIL socket. Note also the different 'pin out' arrangement (Figure 4.19). Other sizes are also available – pin out details should be provided in the catalogue listing them. Whichever size is obtained, do ensure it is the common cathode type.

The display should be easily readable in a normal living room, but in a bright classroom a red filter should be placed over the display. Such filters are available from some electronics suppliers, but the type of material used in stage lighting works very well.

Testing

Connect the supply. Press and release switch S1. A number should appear on the display. If nothing appears, switch off and check for faults. If all is well, press and release S1 several times, to check that a variety of numbers appears.

Fault finding

(Read the section on 'Fault finding' in Chapter 6.)

If the display fails to light at all, check the power supply, especially across IC2. Check the voltage on pin 3 of IC2. It should be nearly equal to the supply. Note that if R2 is 1 MΩ, a good quality voltmeter is required to take an accurate reading. If such a meter is not available, use a temporary wire link to connect pin 3 to positive. If the display still fails to light up, check that its cathode is connected to negative in the circuit. Check also that you have not obtained a 'common anode' display by mistake.

If the display lights up but does not produce recognisable numbers, you have probably mixed up the connections from the outputs of IC2 to the display. Check them carefully.

If the display lights up, but the number fails to change when S1 is pressed, check that pins 2 and 15 of IC2 are correctly connected. It is not easy to check the presence of the clock pulses into pin 1 without using an oscilloscope as described in the previous project. However, a voltage of between 2 and 3 V at pin 1 of IC2 indicates that IC1 is probably producing a clock pulse. If you fail to obtain a correct reading on pin 1 of IC2, check the output at pin 13 of IC1. This should also be between 2 and 3 V if IC1 is working correctly. If this is not the case, check the connections around IC1 very carefully.

Note that it is essential to connect pins 2, 3, 4 and 5 of IC1 to zero (as shown in the layouts) to prevent the spare gates oscillating and either burning out or using too much current.

Experiments and modifications

Making the display light up during counting
If you wish to use the project for timing, or you just want to watch the numbers changing, a simple alteration will make the display stay on all the time. First insert a new wire link (on the breadboard or stripboard) to join pin 3 of IC2 to the positive supply. (On the stripboard layout place the new link from hole A19 to hole D19.) Now cut or remove the wire linking pins 2 and 3 of IC2 together.

You should now find that the display remains on when S1 is pressed. Since it is counting very quickly, all the segments will be flashing faster than you can observe and the display will appear to show an '8'.

Slowing down the counting rate
Assuming that you have made the modification above, you may now wish to slow down the counting rate in order to observe the numbers changing. The counting rate is determined by the frequency of the clock pulse, which in turn is controlled by the values of resistor R1 and capacitor C1.

To reduce the counting speed, either R1 or

C1 or both must be increased in value. Since an electrolytic capacitor is not recommended for C1, it is not easy to increase it by much above the present value. Thus R1 must be increased. However, this is only possible if IC1 is a CMOS type (i.e. 74HC02). Providing this is so, R1 may be increased to 10 MΩ. (Yes, 10 million!) At this value the positive pulses will occur at just over one second intervals.

If R1 is replaced by a potentiometer or preset, the counting rate may be varied more easily. It is difficult to obtain a pot. or preset of more than about 2 MΩ, and you may have to increase C1 to 0.47 μF to enable a counting rate of 1 per second to be set. Also connect a fixed resistor of about 1 MΩ in series with the pot. or preset. It should now be possible to set an interval of exactly 1 second between counts. The project will now form the basis of a timer (especially if extra 4026BE ICs and displays are cascaded), though it may not be particularly accurate. It is possible to design ways of making the timer start and stop automatically in order to time, for example, an object falling.

Manual resetting
The circuit may be reset to zero by applying a positive pulse to pin 15 (reset) of IC2. This can be achieved by connecting a push-to-make switch from positive to pin 15. Resistor R3 must be left in position to hold pin 15 at zero volts at all times except when the new switch is pressed. On the breadboard and stripboard layouts the connecting points required for this push switch are marked with a letter 'P'.

Automatic resetting at switch on
At present, the display may indicate any number when power is switched on. This is not always convenient, especially if using the project to count from zero. Automatic resetting is achieved by connecting a capacitor (C3) from positive to pin 15 (reset). In other words, the same points as the push switch for manual resetting, marked with a 'P' on the layouts. The capacitor will apply a positive pulse to pin 15 at the moment when power is switched on. This pulse, though brief, is enough to make the IC reset to zero.

Note that R3 must still be connected as shown, to hold pin 15 at zero volts after the pulse is received. The extra push switch and the capacitor C3 may both be connected if desired.

Reaction timer
The 'Door bell timer' project earlier in this chapter may be linked with this circuit to produce a reaction timer. Both circuits must share the same battery or power supply.

Begin by setting up the counter so that it counts in tenths of a second. Pin 3 of IC2 should either be connected to pin 2 (as before) or joined to positive as described above. A push switch should be added to the counter circuit to enable IC2 to be reset to zero (as described above).

Pin 2 of IC2 should now be connected to pin 13 of the IC in the 'door bell timer'. Resistor R2 in the counter circuit, must be left in place. The buzzer (in the door bell timer) may be left connected, or replaced with a LED and series resistor if more convenient.

First press the door bell timer switch, and zero the counter. When the buzzer stops sounding, the seven segment display will start counting. Press the door bell timer switch again, as quickly as possible. The display will 'freeze', showing your reaction time.

You may think of a number of refinements to improve the ease with which the circuit is operated. Since the door bell timer requires only two logic gates, you could use the two spare gates of IC1 in the random number display to act as a timer. Take care when selecting the required pins of the IC — a full 'pin out' diagram is shown on page 9.

5 COMPUTER INTERFACING

Three circuits are described which allow a computer to 'communicate' directly with other electronic devices. If the thought of connecting circuits directly to your computer seems daunting, don't be put off! The interfaces are very simple, and various checks can be made to ensure that you do not harm the computer. Probably the hardest part is finding and fitting the correct connector!

The first project is a **computer input interface**. This allows an electrical signal to input directly into the computer and influence a program in some way. Any of the projects described in this book which drive a LED, buzzer or relay may be connected via this interface. The circuit will work with any computer which has a **'user port'**. Full connecting details and programs are included for the Research Machines 380Z, 480Z and BBC 'B' computers.

The second project is a **computer output interface**. This enables the computer to switch on a LED or a relay — which in turn can switch on any electrical apparatus. The output interface may be combined with the input interface. This opens up many possibilities. For example, the input interface may be connected to either light sensor described in this book. As darkness approaches the computer will print a message on the screen, or play a tune (in the case of the BBC or 480Z) and/or switch on a light etc. Full connecting details and example programs are included for the 380Z, 480Z and BBC 'B' computers.

Both the above circuits interface with a *single* channel. The computers mentioned will allow up to eight channels to be interfaced. Thus, if more than one channel is required, additional circuits may be constructed — on one large piece of stripboard if preferred. In this case it is necessary to fully understand how the user port is programmed. This is explained later in this chapter. However, a knowledge of the binary system

(described in Chapter 6) is also essential and many readers may prefer to use just one input and one output channel for the time being at least. In this case the details and simple programs described here may be followed without understanding how they work!

The third project is for the BBC 'B' computer only, and uses its **analogue input**. The simple project described turns the computer into a thermometer. Keen programmers may introduce colourful graphics, or write a program which causes the computer to perform a calculation or switch on (or off) an appliance via the output interface.

Computer Input Interface

Components

Semiconductors
IC1 single opto transistor isolator
D1 diode 1N4001

Resistors (any type)
R1 120 Ω (brown, red, brown, 'any') for 4.5
to 6 V input
   or 270 Ω (red, violet, brown, 'any') for 9
to 12 V input
R2 1.2 kΩ (brown, red, red, 'any')

Miscellaneous
stripboard (0.1 in pitch) about 4 cm by 2 cm
  (not BB) (at least 14 holes by 5 tracks)
IC socket, 6 pin (not BB)
  (an 8 pin socket may be used if a 6 pin is
  difficult to obtain)
suitable connector for computer (see below)
insulated connecting wire

Computer connectors

The Research Machines 380Z and 480Z
require a 25 way 'D' series **plug**. Various
types are available. Purchase one to which
the wires can be soldered. Note that the
metal or plastic covers must be bought
separately.

The BBC computer requires an **insulation displacement connector**' (IDC),
which must be a **2 × 10 way DIL (dual-in-line) socket**. A 20 way ribbon cable is
normally connected to such a socket. The
ribbon cable is placed inside the two halves
of the socket, which are then squeezed
together. This is quite difficult without a
special tool, and the services of a vice may be
necessary! Take care, however, not to crack
the connector. As the connector is squeezed,
the connecting pins pierce the insulation
covering the ribbon cable and all 20 connections are made together.

This method is fast and convenient – if you
require 20 connections. However, in this
circuit only 3 or 4 connections are required
and some readers may prefer an attempt at
soldering the wires directly to the pins of the
socket.

How it works

Computers are expensive and fairly easily
damaged – particularly if a supply above 5 V
is connected into an input. Fortunately, a
device known as an **opto isolator** is available, which provides total isolation for the
computer – up to about 4000 V!

An opto isolator consists of an infrared
LED (a LED which gives out infrared light
instead of visible light), placed close to a
silicon phototransistor (a transistor which
may be turned on by a beam of light). The
LED and phototransistor are housed in the
same plastic case and look like the DIL

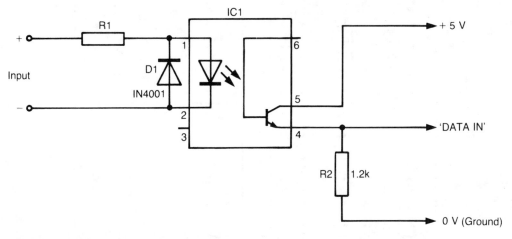

Figure 5.1 Computer input interface: circuit diagram
(Input voltages 4.5 to 6 V: R1 = 120 Ω)
(Input voltages 9 to 12 V: R1 = 270 Ω)

integrated circuits used in earlier chapters. Numerous versions of opto isolators are available. For example, dual opto isolators, quad opto isolators and other varieties for special applications.

When a supply of between 4.5 and 12 V is connected to the 'input', current flows via R1 through the LED inside IC1 (Figure 5.1). R1 reduces the flow of current to a safe level — and the value should be chosen to suit the input voltage being used. For example, for inputs from 4.5 V to 6 V, R1 should be 120 Ω;

for 9 V to 12 V, R1 should be 270 Ω. In practice you may find that, with R1 equal to 270 Ω, the device may still work with an input as low as 5 V, but this is not guaranteed.

Diode D1 protects the LED if the input is connected with the wrong polarity (i.e. the wrong way round). This is necessary, as otherwise the LED may burn out. Diode D1 prevents the reverse voltage across the LED rising to a dangerous level.

It should be apparent that no current from

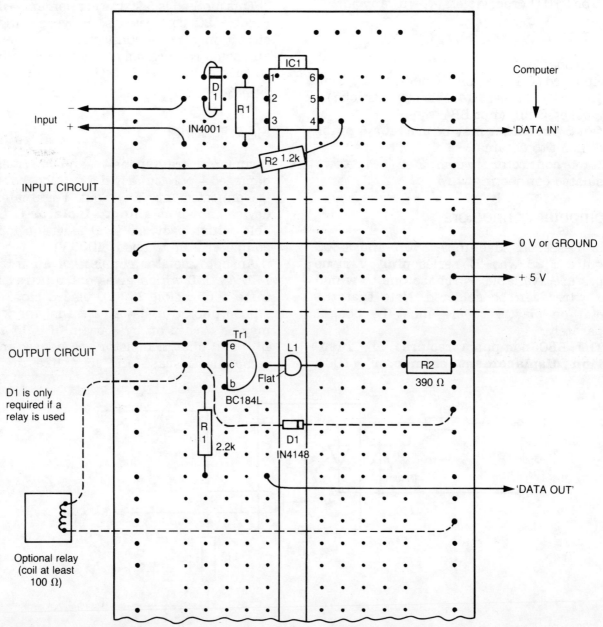

Figure 5.2 Computer input and output interface: layout diagram for breadboard construction
(Note: You may build the input, or the output or both.)

the input can reach pins 4, 5 and 6 and thus damage the computer. When the input current flows, a beam of infrared light from the LED crosses to the transistor. This causes the transistor to switch on, and current flows from the computer's positive 5 V supply, making the voltage at 'DATA IN' 'high' (nearly 5 V). When the input is switched off, the transistor turns off and resistor R2 causes the voltage at 'DATA IN' to fall to zero. Thus a variety of voltages at the input can be used to switch 'DATA IN' from 'low' to 'high' without any direct electrical connection between the input and computer.

Breadboard construction (Figure 5.2)

Follow the 'input circuit' of Figure 5.2, not forgetting the 0 V and 5 V connections. Fit the link and components in the usual way, taking care to place IC1 with the small dot in the top left-hand corner. Ensure that D1 is fitted the correct way round.

Do not fit the computer connector until the circuit has been tested.

Stripboard construction (Figure 5.3)

1 Begin by labelling the board and breaking the tracks as shown.
2 Fit and solder the IC socket and other components in the usual way, taking care to fit D1 the correct way round.
3 Fit the opto isolator in the IC socket ensuring that the small dot is in the top left-hand corner. Do not fit the computer connector until the circuit has been tested.

Testing

The input interface should be tested *before* connecting it to a computer. Check carefully that the tracks have been broken between the pins of the IC. Failure to do this will result in the input connecting directly with the computer.

Connect a voltmeter (or LED and series resistor) between the zero volts line and 'DATA IN'. Connect a 5 V (or 4.5 V) supply to '+5 V' and 'ground' on the computer side. The voltmeter should read 0 V. Connect another supply (e.g. a 9 V battery) to the 'input'. The voltmeter should indicate nearly 5 V.

Fault finding

(Read the section on 'Fault finding' in Chapter 6.)

There are so few components that a visual check should discover a simple fault. Ensure that diode D1 is connected the correct way round, and that the IC is fitted with the small dot near the point where the diode joins the resistor. Check that the breaks have been made properly.

Using the interface

In practice, the input may be connected to a battery of suitable voltage via a switch — for testing. It may also be connected to many of the circuits in this book, in which case the 'input positive' should connect with the positive supply on the circuit, and the 'input negative' should connect to the transistor collector. Figure 5.4 illustrates one example to clarify this.

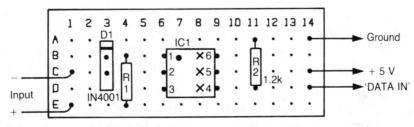

X = breaks in tracks (3 altogether)

Figure 5.3 Computer input interface: layout diagram for stripboard construction
(Note: D1 is connected to tracks B and C.)

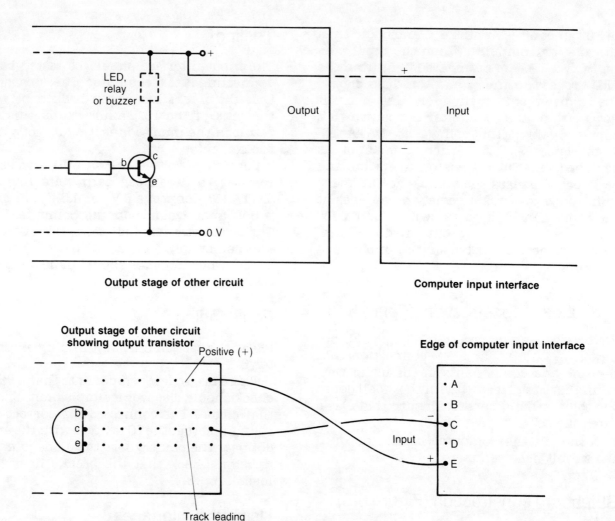

Output stage of other circuit

Computer input interface

Output stage of other circuit showing output transistor

Edge of computer input interface

Positive (+)

Track leading to transistor collector

Figure 5.4 Connecting the computer input interface to another circuit
(Note: The actual tracks may not be as shown.)

Computer input

It may be no surprise to learn that the three computers mentioned all have different operating methods for their user ports. To simplify matters, only brief details will be given at this stage; fuller details will follow later. The 380Z and 480Z machines have similar input connections, but the BBC uses a different type of connector, found underneath the machine.

Connecting to a computer

Having obtained a suitable connector as described earlier, follow Figure 5.5 very carefully and connect the interface circuit. Disregard the 'DATA OUT' connection for now. Make sure that the computer is switched off and nothing is connected to your interface input. Leave the TV or monitor switched on, to ensure that you will be aware of any fault immediately the computer is switched on. Plug in the interface to the user port. Switch on the computer. Watch the TV screen for the normal computer message. If it fails to appear, switch off the computer immediately and check for faults.

Programming

The 380Z uses the command PEEK to ascertain whether an input from the user port is 'high' or 'low'. The 480Z requires the command INP, and the BBC computer uses a

RESEARCH MACHINES 380Z AND 480Z

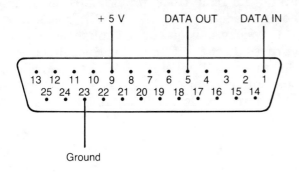

25 way 'D' series plug (plugged into 'USER I/O')

BBC 'B' COMPUTER

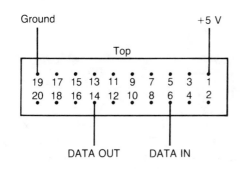

Insulation displacement connector (2 × 10 DIL socket)
(plugged into 'user port')

Figure 5.5 Computer connections (both connectors are viewed from the cable entry side)

'byte indirection operator' — a question mark. The computer must be told an **I/O register number** as the user port is one of many sources of information the computer can access. The I/O register numbers are as follows:

380Z: 64511 480Z: 29 BBC: 65120

The 380Z and 480Z have eight **data input lines** and eight **data output lines**. The BBC has eight **data lines** which can be inputs or outputs (or a mixture). Thus the BBC requires another command to set the lines to input or output. Full details are explained later, but the command '?65122=0' sets all eight lines to 'input'.

Thus to access the user port and print the result on the screen, the following command must be typed.

380Z
PRINT PEEK(64511)

480Z
PRINT INP(29)

BBC
?65122=0
PRINT ?65120

A simple program can now be written, which continually examines the user port and prints the result on the screen. Try the following:

380Z
10 LET P=PEEK(64511)
20 PRINT P
30 GOTO 10

480Z
10 LET P=INP(29)
20 PRINT P
30 GOTO 10

BBC
 5 ?65122=0
10 LET P=65120
20 PRINT P
30 GOTO 10

You should obtain the value 244 with no input to the interface, and the value 255 with the input 'high'. Note that if the interface is unplugged from the computer the value 255 is obtained, as circuits inside the computer make the inputs 'high'.

Using the variable 'P' opens up other possibilities; for example, line 20 could be as follows:

20 IF P=255 THEN PRINT "YOUR DEVICE IS ON" ELSE PRINT "YOUR DEVICE IS OFF"

Using the interface and circuits previously described will enable the computer to detect changes in light, temperature and moisture. If you want the computer to react to several inputs at virtually the same time, you will need to build several input interfaces and understand exactly how the user port works. This is described after the next project.

Computer Output Interface

Components

Semiconductors
Tr1   transistor BC184L
D1   diode 1N4148 (needed only if relay is used)
L1   LED 10 mA, red

Resistors (any type)
R1   2.2 kΩ (red, red, red, 'any')
R2   390 Ω (orange, white, brown, 'any')

Miscellaneous
a relay may be required (see below)
stripboard 4 cm by 2 cm (not BB)
  (at least 14 holes by 7 tracks)
wires
suitable connector for computer (see below)

The details concerning the computer connector are given after the components list for the computer input interface. If you intend using both the input and output interfaces together, they must share the same computer connector.

If you intend using only a LED to indicate an output from the computer, the diode may be omitted.

If a relay is required, D1 must be included (unless already fitted inside the relay). Most 6 V relays will work on 5 V, but ensure that the coil resistance is at least 100 Ω. Reed relays are particularly suitable as they have higher coil resistances. Bear in mind that the computer's 5 V supply has a limited current output. If several output interfaces are required it would be wise to use an external power supply, i.e. a 5 V supply connected as shown. In this case the wire joining the output interface to the computer's +5 V output should be disconnected.

How it works

Each 'Data out' line from the computer can be logic 'high' (nearly 5 V) or logic 'low' (nearly 0 V). When 'low', the voltage at the base of Tr1 is less than 0.6 V, and Tr1 is switched off. Thus no current can flow from positive via the LED or relay (if fitted). When the 'Data out' line goes 'high', the transistor is turned on, and hence the LED lights and/or the relay switches on. Diode D1 protects the transistor against back e.m.f. produced by the relay.

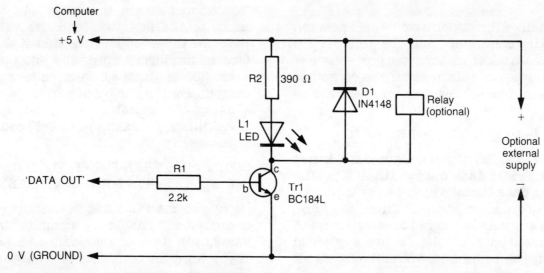

Figure 5.6 Computer output interface: circuit diagram
(Note: Disconnect the computer's +5 V supply lead before using the external supply.)

Breadboard construction (Figure 5.2)

Follow the 'output circuit' of Figure 5.2, not forgetting the 0 V and 5 V connections. Fit the wire link and resistors followed by the transistor and LED, which must be the correct way round. Fit the diode if required, the correct way round. Test the circuit *before* connecting to the computer.

Stripboard construction (Figure 5.7)

Label the board as usual, and take care to fit Tr1, D1 (if required) and L1 the correct way round. Test the circuit *before* connecting to the computer.

Testing

Connect a 5 V (or 4.5 V) supply to the circuit. The LED should not light up. Touch the 'Data out' lead against the positive supply. The LED should light. Do not connect to a computer unless the circuit is working perfectly.

Fault finding

(Read the section on 'Fault finding' in Chapter 6.)

Begin by checking the 5 V supply across the appropriate points in the circuit. Check that diode D1 (if fitted) is the correct way round. If it is facing the wrong way it could damage the transistor and even the computer's 5.V supply. Try shorting the collector and emitter leads of the transistor together. The LED should light, otherwise R2 or the LED is probably at fault. Assuming it did light, the fault must be around R1 or the transistor itself.

Connecting to a computer

Connect the interface to the computer connector according to Figure 5.5. Disregard the 'Data in' connection. If you have already connected the input interface, use the same connector for the output interface.

Programming

The same I/O register numbers are used for the input and output lines. To set the eight BBC lines to output, the command '?65122=255' must be typed. The 380Z computer uses the command 'POKE' to set an output line. The 480Z uses the command 'OUT' and the BBC uses a question mark again. Assuming that you have wired the output interface to the computer connector exactly as illustrated in Figure 5.5 the following command(s) should turn on the LED.

380Z
POKE 64511,1

480Z
OUT 29,1

BBC
?65122=255
?65120=16

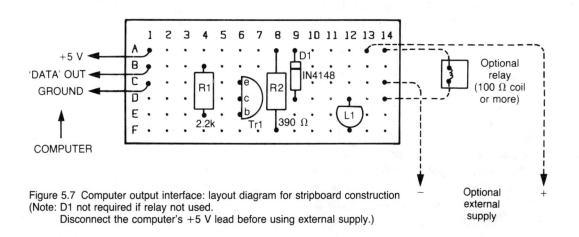

Figure 5.7 Computer output interface: layout diagram for stripboard construction
(Note: D1 not required if relay not used.
Disconnect the computer's +5 V lead before using external supply.)

In the 380Z and 480Z the first number is the I/O register. This must be followed by a comma, then the value to be placed at the user port. The value '1' causes the first line (called **data zero**) to go 'high'. The I/O register for the BBC is 65120. As the 'data zero' line was used as an input in the previous circuit, the fifth line (data 4) has been chosen as an output. The value needed to make data 4 go 'high' is 16. The value 0 will turn off the LED in all three computers.

Thus the following program may be used to test the interface fully:

380Z

```
10  PRINT "Type 1 for ON, 0 for OFF"
20  INPUT X
30  POKE 64511,X
40  GOTO 10
```

480Z

```
10  PRINT "Type 1 for ON, 0 for OFF"
20  INPUT X
30  OUT 29,X
40  GOTO 10
```

BBC

```
 5  ?65122=255
10  PRINT "Type 16 for ON, 0 for OFF"
20  INPUT X
30  ?65120=X
40  GOTO 10
```

Using the input and output interfaces

If you still have the input interface connected to the computer, it should still be working normally with the 380Z and 480Z machines. However, the BBC computer will not accept an input, as the command '?65122=255' sets *all* the data lines to output. To allow both interfaces to work with the BBC, line 5 should be '?65122=240'. This will set the lowest four data lines to input, and the highest four to output. Now both interfaces should work correctly.

The programs listed in Figure 5.8 show one way in which the input interface can be used by the computer to display a message on the screen and switch on the output interface.

```
RESEARCH MACHINES 380Z:

10 REM 380Z INPUT & OUTPUT
20 LET Q=0
30 LET P=PEEK(64511)
40 IF P=Q THEN 30
50 LET Q=P
60 IF P=255 THEN 110
70 PRINT:PRINT"Your device is not active"
80 PRINT"  I shall switch the light OFF"
90 POKE 64511,0
100 GOTO 30
110 PRINT:PRINT"Your device is now active"
120 PRINT"  I shall switch the light ON"
130 POKE 64511,1
140 GOTO 30
```

```
RESEARCH MACHINE 480Z:

10 REM 480Z INPUT & OUTPUT
20 LET Q=0
30 LET P=INP(29)
40 IF P=Q THEN 30
50 LET Q=P
60 IF P=255 THEN 110
70 PRINT:PRINT"Your device is not active"
80 PRINT"  I shall switch the light OFF"
90 OUT 29,0
100 GOTO 30
110 PRINT:PRINT"Your device is now active"
120 PRINT"  I shall switch the light ON"
130 OUT 29,1
140 GOTO 30
```

```
BBC COMPUTER:

10 REM BBC INPUT & OUTPUT
20 LETQ=0
30 ?65122=240
40 LET P=?65120
50 IF P=Q OR P=Q+16 OR P=Q-16 THEN 40
60 LET Q=P
70 IF P=15 OR P=31 THEN 120
80 PRINT:PRINT"Your device is not active"
90 PRINT"  I shall switch the light OFF"
100 ?65120=0
110 GOTO 40
120 PRINT:PRINT"Your device is now active"
130 PRINT"  I shall switch the light ON"
140 ?65120=16
150 GOTO 40
```

Figure 5.8 Computer input/output interface programs

Advanced Use of the User Port

The 380Z and 480Z computers allow up to eight inputs and eight outputs. The BBC computer allows a mixture of inputs and outputs to a combined total of eight. To make best use of these ports a full understanding of the system used is necessary. A knowledge of the **binary system** (see Chapter 6) is required in order to understand this section. The method of outputting will be considered first.

380Z and 480Z computers

An output is achieved using 'POKE' or 'OUT' followed by the input/output register, then a comma, then the output number.

e.g.   POKE 64511,5 (380Z)
       OUT 29,5   (480Z)

The output number (5 in this example) is typed as a decimal. However, the computer converts it to an 8 bit binary number, and each bit corresponds to an output or input data line. If a bit is a '0', the line is 'low', if the bit is a '1' the line is 'high'. To illustrate this take the output number 5. Converted to 8 bit binary: this is 00000101. The following table shows how the data output lines would then be set:

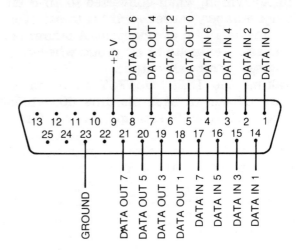

RESEARCH MACHINES 380Z & 480Z

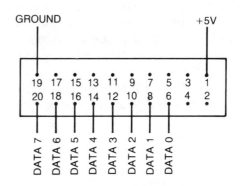

BBC 'B' COMPUTER

Figure 5.9 Full details for the advanced use of the user ports (both connectors are viewed from the cable entry side)
(Note: In all cases the first input/output is called DATA 0 and the eighth is called DATA 7.)

DATA LINE:	7	6	5	4	3	2	1	0
BINARY NUMBER:	0	0	0	0	0	1	0	1
VOLTAGE ON LINE:	low	low	low	low	low	high	low	high

Thus data lines 0 and 2 would go 'high', the other lines remaining 'low'. The relationship between the data lines and the actual pins in the computer connector is illustrated in Figure 5.9.

In the same way, the output number 15 (binary 00001111) will turn on the lowest four data lines; output number 240 (binary 11110000) will turn on the highest four, and 255 (binary 11111111) will turn on all eight data lines. Thus any combination of outputs can be set up with the appropriate output number.

BBC computer

The BBC user port has a total of eight lines which must first be set up as inputs or outputs or a combination of both. A **data direction register** is used for this purpose, and is located at address 65122. To set up the data direction register, the command

'?65122=K' is used, where 'K' is a decimal number which, when converted to an 8 bit binary number, causes each bit to set each data line as an input or output. A binary bit '0' causes the line to be an input, whereas a '1' causes it to be an output.

Taking the INPUT/OUTPUT program in Figure 5.8 as an example, line 30, which reads '?65122=240', sets up data lines 0 to 3 as inputs, and data lines 4 to 7 as outputs. This is because the decimal number 240 equals binary 11110000. To set up alternate inputs and outputs the binary number required would be 10101010. This is equivalent to decimal 170. Thus the BBC command would be ?65122=170. If six inputs and two outputs were required, the six inputs could be grouped together from data lines 0 to 5, leaving data lines 6 and 7 as the outputs. This would require binary 11000000, which equals decimal 192. The command ?65122=192 would thus be required.

Having set the data direction register, the actual output is set up in a similar way to the 380Z and 480Z. The input/output register is 65120, and this is placed after a question mark as follows:

$$?65120=5$$

This would turn on data lines 0 and 2, since 5 equals binary 00000101.

Input interface

The logic involved in allowing the computer to register an input is very similar. The 380Z and 480Z computers use the commands PEEK and INP respectively. This is followed by the input/output register in brackets.

e.g. LET P=PEEK(64511) (380Z)
      LET P=INP(29)   (480Z)

In both cases, P becomes a decimal number based on the binary equivalent determined by which input data lines were 'high' or 'low'. For example, if data lines 0, 2 and 5 were 'high' and the others low, the binary number would be 00100101, and P would equal 37.

The equivalent command for the BBC is:

$$LET\ P=?65122$$

Before typing this line in a program it would be necessary to set up the BBC's data direction register as described earlier.

In all three computers it should be noted that any data line which is acting as an input will rise to nearly 5 V if left unconnected. Thus, in the examples above, P will equal the decimal number 255 (binary 11111111) if nothing is connected to the user input.

Switching Outputs On and Off Independently

The following applies to all three computers. If you have built several output interfaces and tried to control them with the computer you may have found a problem. For example, data output line 4 requires binary 00010000, which is decimal 16. If you then wish to turn on data output 5 as well, you may have typed decimal 32. Unfortunately, data output 4 will have switched off, since decimal 32 equals binary 00100000. Notice that the fifth digit from the right (data 4) is now '0'. The number you require to switch on data outputs 4 and 5 is 48 (binary 00110000). Switching on or off even more outputs becomes very complicated and difficult to program. Fortunately the **logical operators** 'OR' and 'AND' come to the rescue.

Logical operators enable individual data lines to be controlled without changing the other data lines. Taking the 'OR' operator first, it is similar to the action of the 'OR' logic gates described in Chapter 6.

```
e.g. 0 OR 0 = 0
     0 OR 1 = 1
     1 OR 0 = 1
     1 OR 1 = 1
```

The computer may be used to examine their action using the command "PRINT". For example, type:

PRINT 0 OR 1

The computer responds with 1. This is because the two numbers in 8 bit binary are compared bit by bit. Thus the total result of:

```
   00000000
OR 00000001
=  00000001
```

The two numbers are treated rather like an addition sum, except that *no numbers are carried*.

Try another example. Type:

PRINT 8 OR 16

Converted to binary, this becomes:

```
   00001000   (decimal 8)
OR 00010000   (decimal 16)
=  00011000   which equals decimal 24
```

It may appear that the two numbers are simply added together. This is not the case, as illustrated in the next example:

PRINT 24 OR 10

Converted to binary:

```
   00011000   (decimal 24)
OR 00001010   (decimal 10)
=  00011010   which equals decimal 26
```

Remembering that the '1's represent the data outputs switched on, this method enables extra outputs to be switched on without affecting the state of other outputs. To switch on an additional output it is only necessary to make the computer examine the user port to establish which outputs are already on (using PEEK, INP or ?), and then combine this with the new instruction using 'OR'. For example, suppose we wish to switch on data output 3 in addition to any other outputs already on. Data output 3 is represented by binary 00001000, which is decimal 8. The command would therefore be:

380Z
POKE 64511, PEEK(64511) OR 8

480Z
OUT 29, INP(29) OR 8

BBC
?65120=?65120 OR 8

It is equally important to be able to switch off a data output without affecting other outputs. The logical operator 'AND' may be used. The principle is similar to an AND logic gate, where:

```
0 AND 0 = 0
0 AND 1 = 0
1 AND 0 = 0
1 AND 1 = 1
```

Testing this with a computer again, try typing the simple examples above. Then try:

PRINT 8 AND 16

Converted to binary:

```
    00001000  (decimal 8)
AND 00010000  (decimal 16)
=   00000000  which equals decimal 0
```

Now try:

PRINT 24 AND 8

Converted to binary, and applying 'AND' to each bit:

```
    00011000  (decimal 24)
AND 00001000  (decimal 8)
=   00001000  which equals decimal 8
```

In order to switch off a particular output, the required decimal number must be subtracted from 255 (binary 11111111). If, for example, you have data outputs 3 and 4 'high' (binary 00011000 = decimal 24), and you wish to switch off only output 3 (decimal 8), type:

PRINT 24 AND 255−8

```
    00011000  (decimal 24)
AND 11110111  (decimal 255−8)
=   00010000  which equals decimal 16
```
(data output 4)

Suppose several data outputs are switched on, and you wish to switch off data output 3 without affecting the others. The computer is instructed to examine the user port (with PEEK, INP or ?) and then made to apply a logical 'AND' to this and the number 8 subtracted from 255. For example:

380Z
POKE 64511, PEEK(64511) AND 255−8

480Z
OUT 29, INP(29) AND 255−8

BBC
?65120=?65120 AND 255−8

Most people find this type of computer work heavy going at first. If you have become confused or lost, experiment with the computer and read through this part again, section by section. Eventually the mist will clear!

BBC Computer Thermometer

This project is only suitable for use with the BBC 'B' computer. It is possible, however, to display the temperature on a good quality voltmeter (instead of a computer). The voltmeter should be able to display millivolts to three significant figures; a digital type is ideal.

Components

Semiconductors
IC1 semiconductor temperature sensor type 590KH

Resistors
R1   910 Ω (any type) (white, brown, brown, 'any')
VR1 preset, min. horizontal, 100 Ω

Miscellaneous
stripboard 4 cm by 1.5 cm (not BB) (at least 14 holes by 6 tracks)
15 way 'D' connecting plug
insulated connecting wires

How it works

This circuit (Figure 5.10) requires very few components and, as you may expect, a very clever integrated circuit is employed. The IC will operate on any voltage from 4 to 30 V, and acts like a constant current regulator. In other words, the voltage across the IC does not affect the current flowing through it. The *temperature* of the IC does affect the current. Not only does the current change, but it changes in exact proportion with the temperature.

The thermistor used in an earlier project behaved in similar fashion except that the changing current was not in direct proportion to the temperature. In other words, it was 'non linear'. While the thermistor could be used to make the circuit react at a certain temperature, its non linearity would have presented enormous problems had the circuit been required to give a wide range of temperature readings.

Returning to this circuit, it is important to note that the current flowing through the IC varies in direct proportion with the temperature measured in **degrees Kelvin**. This is the 'absolute temperature scale' which begins at absolute zero (the lowest temperature possible), and rises in direct proportion with the Celsius scale. Absolute zero (0 K) is equal to $-273.2\,°C$. (For simplicity we will call this $-273\,°C$.) The comparison in the table on p. 112 should make this clear.

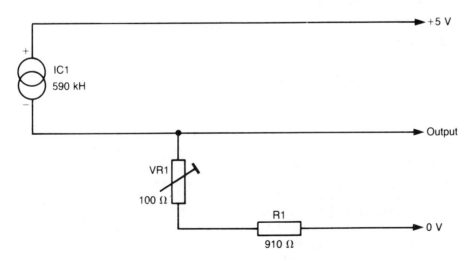

Figure 5.10 BBC computer thermometer: circuit diagram

°C	K	
100	373	boiling point of pure water
37	310	normal body temperature
20	293	comfortable room temperature
0	273	freezing point of pure water
−273	0	absolute zero

Thus to convert from degrees Kelvin to degrees Celsius, simply subtract 273. Since the project is intended for use with a computer, the computer program can be made to do this automatically, or it could display both Kelvin and Celsius readings.

The positive input to IC1 is connected to the computer's +5 V supply. The 'negative' side of the IC is connected to VR1 and R1 in series. Current flowing via the IC flows through these resistances and causes a voltage at the junction between the IC and VR1. This voltage will vary in direct proportion to the current, and hence the temperature of the IC. (See Ohm's Law, page 117.)

If VR1 is set so that the total combined resistance with R1 is 1000 Ω, the voltage (in millivolts) at the output will equal the temperature of the IC in degrees Kelvin. Taking an example, if the IC is placed in melting ice at 0 °C, the equivalent absolute temperature is 273 K, and the voltage at the output will be 273 mV (or 0.273 V). At a room temperature of 20 °C (293 K), the output will rise to 293 mV (0.293 V).

Computer analogue port

Microcomputers normally work with binary digits (hence the name 'digital computer'). Binary digits are either 1's or 0's; on's or off's. A varying voltage is meaningless — it must be either 'high' or 'low'. Converting a varying voltage into a binary number can be accomplished with a fairly complicated IC. Such an IC is built into the BBC 'B' computer. This is called an **analogue to digital converter**. An analogue voltage, which may be between 0 and 1.8 V in the case of the BBC 'B', is converted into a digital value by this IC.

Each analogue to digital conversion takes a fraction of a second to complete. If the voltage is rising or falling quickly, it is important to complete as many conversions every second as possible. Fortunately, speed is not a problem in this circuit, since temperature changes quite slowly.

There are four analogue inputs — labelled (confusingly again) 0 to 3. The four analogue input pins, plus some others, are found within the 'analogue in' connector at the rear of the computer. This project should normally be connected to the first analogue channel (channel 0) which is pin 15 on the connector.

In a computer program, channel 0 is accessed and printed on the screen by the command PRINT ADVAL(1). A number between 0 and 65520 will be printed which corresponds to a voltage ranging from 0 to 1.8 V at pin 15. The range from 0 to 65520 is a little misleading, as this value rises in steps of 16. Thus in most programs the ADVAL value is divided by 16, resulting in a range of values from 0 to 4095.

Converting this value to a temperature is a little complicated (mathematically) but is carried out automatically by the computer program listed in Figure 5.11.

Computer program

The value 'V' in line 10 (Figure 5.11) is a reference voltage produced by the computer. This should be 1.8 V but in practice it is not always accurate. This point will be taken up later.

```
 10 LET V=1.8
 20 MODE2
 30 COLOUR1
 40 COLOUR132
 50 CLS
 60 PRINT TAB(1,12);"TEMPERATURE=";
 70 LET R=ADVAL(1)DIV16
 80 LET TK=V*R/4.095
 90 LET TC=TK-273.2
100 LET T=INT(TC+0.5)
110 PRINT TAB(14,12);SPC(5)
120 COLOUR3:PRINT TAB(13,12);T;"C"
130 FOR X=1 TO 600:NEXT
140 GOTO 70
```

Figure 5.11 BBC computer thermometer program

Line 80 converts this reading into a voltage (in millivolts), which equals the temperature in degrees Kelvin. Line 90 converts this temperature to degrees Celsius. Line 100 changes the value to the nearest whole number which is plotted on the screen at line 120. The other lines produce a pleasing screen display.

Breadboard construction (Figure 5.12)

1 Fit VR1, bending the right-hand tag horizontal, and fit resistor R1.
2 Fit IC1, noting that only two of the leads are required. Ensure that it is fitted the correct way round, noting the position of the small tag.
3 *Do not* connect the computer plug for the moment.

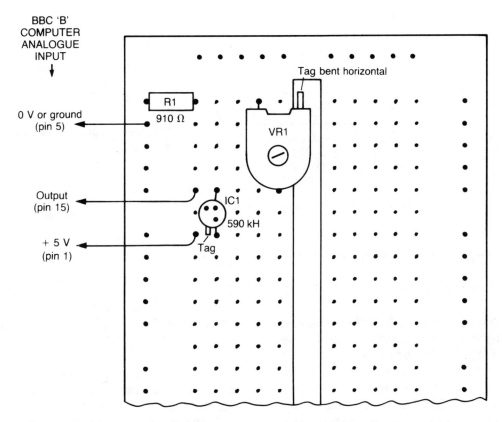

Figure 5.12 BBC computer thermometer: layout diagram for breadboard construction

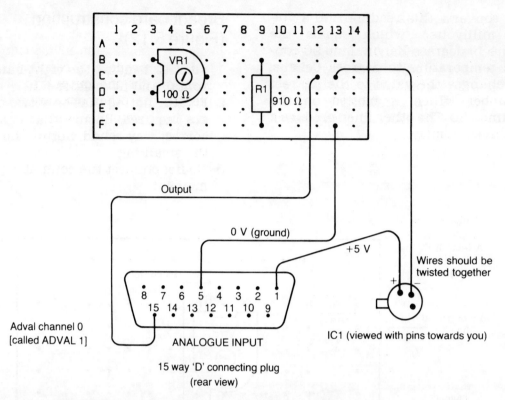

Figure 5.13 BBC computer thermometer: layout diagram for stripboard construction

Stripboard construction (Figure 5.13)

1 Label the board as usual and fit VR1 and R1.
2 IC1 may be fitted directly to the stripboard or via long wires as shown. In this case *ensure that the wires cannot short-circuit as the computer analogue input could be damaged.* Insulate the wires carefully and completely. The IC could be housed at the end of a glass tube with its wires running down the centre. If you wish to measure the temperature of liquids, the IC must be sealed to the glass tube to prevent the liquid reaching the leads.
3 *Do not* connect the computer plug for the moment.

Testing

Connect the positive side of a voltmeter to the 'output' and the negative side to 0 V. Connect a 4.5 or 5 V supply to the circuit. You should obtain a reading of less than 1 V. Adjust VR1 fully one way then the other. Providing you always obtain a reading above zero, and below 1 V, the circuit may be connected to a computer.

If the voltmeter is very accurate it should display a reading in millivolts equal to the temperature of the IC in degrees Kelvin. You could even use this circuit without a computer. Obtain an accurate thermometer and adjust the preset VR1 until the reading in millivolts equals the correct temperature in degrees Kelvin. Alternatively, place the IC in melting ice (taking care not to wet its leads) and adjust VR1 for a reading of 273 mV.

Connecting to the computer

Connect the wires to the computer 15 way 'D' connecting plug and plug in. Switch on the TV before the computer so that any problem will show up immediately on the screen. Switch on the computer and check for the normal message on the screen. If the message does not appear, switch off at once and check for faults.

If all is well, type in the complete program in Figure 5.11. When the program runs, the screen should become blue, and the word "TEMPERATURE =" should appear near the centre, followed by a value and a letter "C". The value will be in degrees Celsius. Follow the procedure in the second paragraph of 'testing' to calibrate the computer thermometer and adjust VR1 until the correct reading is shown.

You may find that VR1 cannot be turned far enough to obtain the correct reading. The reason for this is that the BBC computer does not maintain a very accurate 1.8 V reference by which a comparison is made internally. You can alter the value of V in line 10 of the program to correct this problem. For example, if the temperature displayed is too low, raise the value of V in line 10 to 1.9. This should be more than sufficient. If the temperature displayed is too high, the value of V may be reduced slightly.

The 1.8 (so called) reference voltage is available at pins 11 and 14 of the 'analogue in' connector. You could connect an accurate voltmeter from one of these pins to ground (pin 5) and measure the actual reference voltage. This value may then be placed in line 10 of the program. Note that, as the computer warms up, the reference voltage may change slightly.

There are many applications for this circuit and you may like to change the program to produce a more interesting display. You could make the computer produce a result in degrees Fahrenheit by multiplying the Celsius reading by 1.8 and then adding 32. The computer can also be programmed to plot a graph of temperature against time. Excellent cooling curves are possible with this circuit.

When used in conjunction with the other interfaces, the computer could acquire a variety of information in addition to temperature, and produce a result either on the screen or via the output interface. When linked to the other circuits you may have built, the possibilities for experimentation are endless.

6 FURTHER INFORMATION

Basic Electrical Units

Voltage

Voltage is a term often used for **potential difference**, and can be likened to **pressure** or 'pushing power'. For example, we might say that the voltage of a battery powering a project is 9 **volts** (9 V). This means that the potential difference between its positive (+) and negative (−) terminals is 9 V. Voltage may be measured with a **voltmeter** connected across the battery, or across (in **parallel** with) the component in question, as illustrated in Figure 6.1. When testing a circuit, many of the required measurements may be made with the negative of the voltmeter connected to the negative point in the circuit, the positive voltmeter lead being used as a 'probe' checking voltages around the circuit.

Current

The rate of flow of current through a wire is measured in **amps** (A) (short for amperes). This rate of flow is a measure of the **quantity of electricity flowing per second**. In the same way, you could measure the quantity of water flowing through a pipe in litres per second. Rate of flow of current is measured with an **ammeter** connected in **series** in the circuit, as shown in Figure 6.1.

Power

Electrical power is measured in **watts** (W). Power may be found mathematically by multiplying voltage and current:

$$\text{power} = \text{voltage} \times \text{current}$$

Thus, if a light bulb is designed for operation on 12 volts, and uses 3 amps, its power is given by:

$$\text{power} = 12 \times 3 = 36 \text{ watts}$$

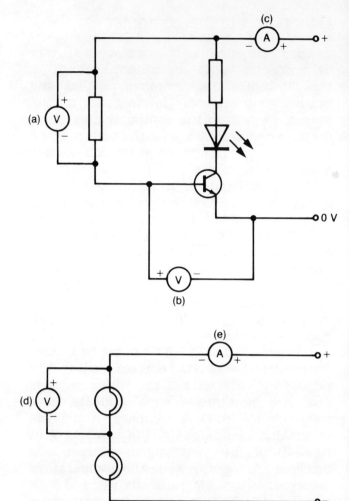

Figure 6.1 (a) Using a voltmeter to measure the voltage across a resistor; (b) using a voltmeter to measure the voltage from zero to the transistor base; (c) using an ammeter to measure the current flowing through the circuit; (d) using a voltmeter to measure the voltage across a bulb; (e) using an ammeter to measure the current flowing through the bulbs

Resistance

Electricity flows easily through a good conductor such as copper. It does not flow as easily through certain other materials, such as nichrome or carbon. This is because nichrome and carbon have a higher resistance. Resistance is measured in **ohms** (often represented by the Greek letter omega, Ω). A short piece of ordinary copper connecting wire may have less than 1 Ω resistance. A similar piece of nichrome wire may have several ohms or tens of ohms resistance. A piece of carbon may have hundreds, thousands or even millions of ohms resistance.

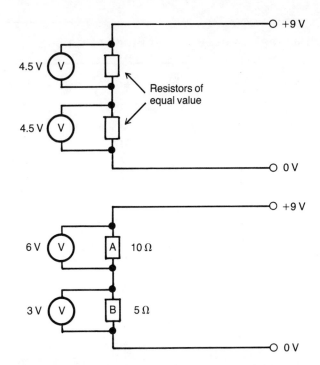

Figure 6.2 Diagram showing how two resistors wired in series can become a potential divider.
(Note: The values 10 Ω and 5 Ω are examples. The same voltages will be obtained for any pair of values, provided that the value of resistor A is twice that of resistor B. In electronic circuits, fairly high values are chosen (to reduce current consumption), e.g. A may be 10 kΩ and B may be 5 kΩ.)

There is an important relationship between voltage, current and resistance. A voltage of 1 volt across a conductor of 1 ohm resistance, will drive a current of 1 amp through. If the voltage is doubled to 2 volts, the current will double to 2 amps. (Twice the voltage will push twice the current through.) This relationship is known as **Ohm's Law** and is fundamental to electricity and electronics. You do not have to understand it to build the projects in this book, but it is essential if you wish to alter or design your own circuit.

Ohm's Law

Ohm's Law states that:

The current flowing through a conductor is directly proportional to the potential difference (voltage) across its ends providing the temperature remains constant.

This leads to the following formula:

$$\text{resistance} = \frac{\text{voltage}}{\text{current}}$$

In other words, resistance equals voltage divided by current.

Resistance is measured in ohms. A conductor has a resistance of 1 ohm if a voltage across it of 1 volt causes a current of 1 amp to flow.

The resistance formula can be rearranged to give:

$$\text{voltage} = \text{current} \times \text{resistance}$$
$$\text{current} = \text{voltage/resistance}$$

Resistors in series

When resistors are connected in **series** (in line, one after another), the total resistance will be *higher* than any one of the resistors by itself. The total is found by *adding* their separate values. For example, a resistor of 3 Ω in series with a resistor of 5 Ω will produce a total resistance of 8 Ω.

Potential dividers

When two (or more) resistors are wired in series, they can become a potential divider (see Figure 6.2). In other words, the voltage is divided between the resistors. Taking an example, if two resistors of equal value are wired across a 9 V supply, there will be a voltage of 4.5 V across each resistor. If a resistance of 10 Ω is connected in series with a resistance of 5 Ω, the voltage across each will be in the ratio 10 to 5, i.e. 2 to 1. Thus with a 9 V supply there will be a voltage of 6 V across the 10 Ω resistor, and 3 V across the 5 Ω resistor.

Resistors in parallel

When resistors are connected in **parallel** (one across another), the total resistance will be *lower* than that of any one of the resistors by itself. The total is more difficult to calculate than with resistors in series, and the following formula may be used for any number of resistors in parallel:

$$\frac{1}{\text{total}} = \frac{1}{A} + \frac{1}{B} + \frac{1}{C} \text{ etc.}$$

where A, B and C are the individual resistor values.

If only *two* resistors are connected in parallel, the formula above may still be used (without $1/C$ of course), or the following, simpler formula may be helpful.

total resistance $= \dfrac{\text{resistances multiplied}}{\text{resistances added}}$

For example, if resistors of $4\,\Omega$ and $6\,\Omega$ are connected in parallel, the total resistance will be:

$$\frac{4 \times 6}{4 + 6} = \frac{24}{10} = 2.4\,\Omega$$

Impedance

The effect of resistance is to impede the flow of current. Inductance (produced by a coil or **inductor**) and capacitance (produced by a capacitor) also behave in a similar way under certain conditions. The general term for this type of opposition to current flow is **reactance**. Reactance is also measured in ohms. When an alternating current is made to flow through a coil or capacitor the combined opposition produced by resistance and reactance is called **impedance**.

For example, loudspeakers work with audio signals which are alternating. Thus the figure in ohms marked on a loudspeaker refers to its impedance.

Binary Numbers

As the name suggests, there are just two binary digits, 0 and 1. Thus two voltage levels may be used to represent binary numbers. These two voltage levels or 'states' are sometimes called 'high' (meaning 1) and 'low' (meaning 0).

Our decimal system employs ten digits (0 to 9). When you reach a count of ten, a '1' is carried into the next column, making the number '10'.

The binary system uses two digits (0 and 1). When you reach a count of two, a '1' is also carried into the next column making the binary number '10'. If one more is added, the binary number becomes '11'. If one more is added to that, the binary number becomes '100'.

Decimal number		Binary number			
10's	1's	8's	4's	2's	1's
	0	0	0	0	0
	1	0	0	0	1
	2	0	0	1	0
	3	0	0	1	1
	4	0	1	0	0
	5	0	1	0	1
	6	0	1	1	0
	7	0	1	1	1
	8	1	0	0	0
	9	1	0	0	1
1	0	1	0	1	0
1	1	1	0	1	1
1	2	1	1	0	0
1	3	1	1	0	1
1	4	1	1	1	0
1	5	1	1	1	1

The table illustrates a set of 4 bit binary numbers. In other words, the binary number has 4 binary digits. Many microcomputers use 8 bit binary numbers. Thus the decimal number 15 would be represented by the 8 bit binary number 00001111. The largest binary number which can be represented in 8 bits is 11111111. This equals decimal 255.

Those mathematically inclined may notice that the numbers at the top of each binary column in the table can be determined in the following way:

$$1\text{'s} = 2^0$$
$$2\text{'s} = 2^1$$
$$4\text{'s} = 2^2$$
$$8\text{'s} = 2^3 \quad \text{etc.}$$

Resistors

Resistors are easily recognised by their coloured bands. There are exceptions, of course, but most small, fixed-value resistors have four or five coloured bands indicating their value.

Resistors reduce the flow of electricity. The amount of resistance is measured in ohms (see page 116). They are often used to limit current and reduce voltage in a circuit.

Many new constructors fail to understand that a resistor will only reduce voltage if current is actually flowing. The amount by which voltage is reduced depends upon the size of the current as well as the resistance. The relationship between voltage, current and resistance is summed up in Ohm's Law. For example, a resistor cannot be used to reduce 12 V to 5 V unless you know exactly what current is flowing. There are far better ways of regulating voltage, as shown in Chapter 3.

Circuit designers calculate each required resistor value, allowing for both voltage and current. The constructor only has to select the value indicated in the circuit.

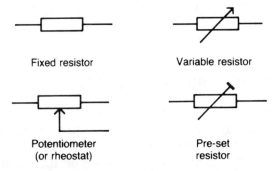

Fixed resistor   Variable resistor

Potentiometer   Pre-set
(or rheostat)   resistor

Figure 6.3 Resistor symbols

Selecting the value

You need not learn or even understand the colour code in order to build the projects in this book, but the system is explained for those wishing to substitute other values or progress to more advanced circuits.

Four band resistors

Hold the resistor so that the band nearest the edge of the resistor is on your left. The fourth band may be spaced a little further away, and on the right. You may have some difficulty at first in holding the resistor the correct way round, especially as the spacing of the four bands varies from make to make. If you purchase the resistors specified in this book, the fourth band will be silver, gold, red or brown. This band should be on the right.

The first three bands represent the value of the resistor in ohms. The fourth band represents the tolerance (i.e. how accurate the value is). Absence of a fourth band indicates a tolerance of 20% (very poor). A silver fourth band indicates 10% (fair); gold represents 5% (good); red 2%; brown 1%. The required tolerance will be indicated on each circuit. You may always use a better (lower percentage) type if desired, but avoid a worse type than specified. The value in ohms is obtained as shown below.

COLOUR	BAND 1 1st digit	BAND 2 2nd digit	BAND 3 multiplier (number of noughts)	BAND 4 tolerance
black	0	0	none	
brown	1	1	0	1%
red	2	2	00	2%
orange	3	3	000	
yellow	4	4	0000	
green	5	5	00000	
blue	6	6	000000	
violet	7	7	0000000	
grey	8	8	00000000	
white	9	9	000000000	
silver			divide by 100	10%
gold			divide by 10	5%

For most purposes, you can think of the multiplier as the number of noughts. On low-value resistors, the third (multiplier) band may be silver or gold. In this case, silver means *divide* by 100; gold means *divide* by 10. Thus the colours RED VIOLET ORANGE GOLD would indicate a value of 2 (red) 7 (violet) 000 (3 noughts – orange) = 27 000 Ω. In other words, a resistor of value 27 000 Ω, and tolerance 5%. This value would normally be written 27 kΩ, since 'k' stands for one thousand. In a similar way, 33 000 000 Ω would be written 33 MΩ, since M stands for one million (meg.).

The following examples may help clarify the system:

BROWN	BLACK	RED	
1	0	00	= 1000 Ω (written 1k)
BROWN	GREEN	RED	
1	5	00	= 1500 Ω (written 1.5k or 1k5)
ORANGE	ORANGE	BROWN	
3	3	0	= 330 Ω (written 330R)
BLUE	GREY	BLACK	
6	8	–	= 68 Ω (written 68R)
YELLOW	VIOLET	BLUE	
4	7	000000	= 47000000 Ω (written 47M)
GREEN	BLUE	GREEN	
5	6	00000	= 5600000 Ω (written 5.6M or 5M6)

Five band resistors
The value of five band resistors is indicated by the first four bands, the fifth, at the other end of the resistor, indicates the tolerance. The system is similar to the one for four band resistors, except that the first three colours represent the first three digits and the fourth is the multiplier. The following examples should clarify the system:

BROWN	BLACK	BLACK	BROWN	
1	0	0	0	= 1000 Ω (1k)
BROWN	GREEN	BLACK	BROWN	
1	5	0	0	= 1500 Ω (1.5k)
ORANGE	ORANGE	BLACK	BLACK	
3	3	0	–	= 330 Ω

Potentiometers/variable resistors

These are often referred to as 'pots'. They are frequently used as volume controls in TVs and radios, and normally have three connections. The centre tag is the wiper, and this is able to traverse from one end of the resistance to the other. Pots. are available with linear (lin.) or logarithmic (log.) tracks. Buying the wrong type will not matter unduly, but log. types are useful in sound applications (amplifiers etc.) to correspond with the way in which the human ear hears sound. Thus, when you increase the volume control, the level of sound appears to increase evenly. Circuit diagrams should specify which type is required.

Presets
A preset is a miniature potentiometer which may be 'preset' to a particular setting. Presets are sold in all shapes and sizes, and plug directly into the stripboard or p.c.b. along with other components. Being small and cheap, they are ideal when you seldom have to change their settings. Presets are only supplied with a linear track.

Power rating

The physical size of a resistor determines the amount of power it can handle. Higher power types are generally more expensive than low-power resistors. Power is measured in watts, or milliwatts (1000 mW = 1 W). You may use a higher power rating than specified in a circuit, providing the resistor will fit in the space allowed, but *never* use a lower power than specified.

Type of material
In most applications the material used is of little importance. In general, resistors will be carbon film, high stability, low-noise types. Alternatively, metal film resistors may be used. These offer a better performance, but you will probably not notice the difference!

Buying guide
When ordering a resistor, check the following:

value (in ohms)	buy the nearest available
tolerance (in percent)	buy that indicated, or better
power (in watts)	buy that indicated, or higher

Capacitors

A capacitor (sometimes called a condenser) is normally designed with two conductors separated by an insulator. In practice, the material used as the insulator affects the task for which the capacitor may be employed. The insulator is called the dielectric, and circuits often specify the type to be used. Examples are: ceramic, carbonate, polystyrene, polyester, etc.

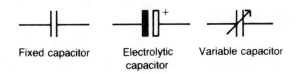

Fixed capacitor   Electrolytic capacitor   Variable capacitor

Figure 6.4 Capacitor symbols

The capacitor is able to store electrical energy. If a battery (direct current supply) is connected to a capacitor, electricity will flow for a fraction of a second until the capacitor is charged. The flow of electricity will then stop. The charged capacitor will now act rather like a battery. However, if connected to a bulb etc., it will probably 'run down' (discharge) in a fraction of a second.

At first, this does not sound very useful. However, the ability of a capacitor to prevent the flow of direct current (d.c.) can be of immense value, e.g. in audio circuits – amplifiers etc. Audio signals alternate backwards and forwards. When fed to a capacitor this type of alternating current (a.c.) will constantly charge and discharge the capacitor. Thus the signal will appear to flow as though the capacitor was an ordinary conductor. Hence the capacitor may be used to block the flow of d.c. between sections of the amplifier, but allow the flow of a.c. (the audio signal). The usefulness of this will be seen in Chapter 3.

Since a capacitor can store electrical energy, it will act in a similar way to the water tank in the loft. The water tank maintains a steady pressure throughout the system – even if the hot taps are turned on. Large-value capacitors are used in a similar way to maintain a steady voltage throughout an electronic circuit. This can often be found in mains driven power supplies, where a smoothing capacitor converts rather rough d.c. into smooth d.c., similar to that obtained from a battery.

Measuring capacitance

Capacitance is measured in farads (F). However, the farad is too large a unit for most practical purposes, and capacitor values are in microfarads (μF), nanofarads (nF), and picofarads (pF). The relationship between these units often confuses newcomers, and the following summary may help:

$$1 \text{ F} = 1\,000\,000 \text{ μF} = 1\,000\,000\,000 \text{ nF}$$
$$= 1\,000\,000\,000\,000 \text{ pF}$$
$$1 \text{ μF} = 1\,000 \text{ nF} = 1\,000\,000 \text{ pF}$$
$$1 \text{ nF} = 1\,000 \text{ pF}$$

To convert from μF to nF, move the decimal point three places to the right: e.g. 0.22 μF = 220 nF.

To convert from nF to pF, move the decimal point three places to the right: e.g. 47 nF = 47 000 pF.

To convert from μF to pF, move the decimal point six places to the right: e.g. 0.001 μF = 1000 pF.

To perform the reverse conversions, move the decimal point the appropriate number of places to the left.

The following is a summary of frequently used values where confusion often arises:

0.0047 μF	= 4.7 nF	= 4700 pF
0.01 μF	= 10 nF	= 10 000 pF
0.022 μF	= 22 nF	= 22 000 pF
0.1 μF	= 100 nF	= 100 000 pF
0.22 μF	= 220 nF	= 220 000 pF
0.47 μF	= 470 nF	= 470 000 pF

Capacitors may be connected in series or in parallel. When two or more are wired in parallel, the total capacitance is found by adding together the individual values. If wired in series, the total capacitance is found using the formula given for resistors in parallel.

Working voltage
When selecting a capacitor, the capacitor's working voltage must be equal to, or higher than, that specified in the circuit diagram. If no such voltage is indicated in the circuit, then this aspect may be disregarded. Small-value capacitors normally have a working voltage many times greater than that required in low-voltage circuits.

Tolerance
A capacitor's tolerance (accuracy) is allowed for when the type is specified in the circuit diagram. Thus tolerance may normally be disregarded.

Type (of dielectric used)
This can be quite important – though selecting the wrong type is unlikely to prevent the circuit working completely. The range of types available can be quite daunting, but if the circuit diagram does not specify a particular type, then select the least expensive.

Very small-value capacitors include disc, ceramic, polystyrene and mica; larger types include polycarbonate, polyester and mylar. These capacitors are commonly available in values to a little over 2 μF. Beyond this, the physical size would become very large, and a totally different type of capacitor is normally used.

Buying guide
When ordering, quote the *type, value* and, sometimes, *voltage* required.

Electrolytic capacitors

These range in value from a fraction of 1 μF, to 10 000 μF or more. The high values offered make them ideal in smoothing circuits, but their working voltages are much lower than non electrolytic types, and must be watched carefully when placing an order.

Unlike ordinary capacitors, electrolytic types must be connected the correct way round – that is, the positive (+) of the capacitor must be connected towards positive in the circuit, and negative (−) of the capacitor towards negative.

Tantalum bead capacitors are sometimes specified. These are similar, except that they offer large values in very small packages. They may also be more expensive.

Style
Electrolytic capacitors are available with a wire at each end (called axial lead electrolytics), or with the two wires at the same end (called single-ended electrolytics). The latter type is ideal for printed circuit boards and stripboards, as they may be mounted vertically, thus saving space. The axial lead types may be mounted horizontally (i.e. flat against the board), or one wire may be bent right round the body of the capacitor to enable vertical mounting. Some complex circuits specify the type required, particularly if space is limited; normally however, it makes little difference.

Buying guide
When ordering, quote the *style, value* and *voltage* required.

Variable capacitors

As the name suggests, this type of capacitor may be varied in value. The range offered may be from zero to a few hundred pico farads. They are often used for tuning in radio etc. Variable capacitors are quite expensive, but cheaper miniature versions are available, called trimmers.

Buying guide
When ordering, quote the *style* and *value* required.

Semiconductor Diodes

A semiconductor diode is a device which allows current to flow in only one direction. In other words, it has a *low forward resistance*, and a *high reverse resistance*. It is essential to connect a diode the *correct way round* as shown in the circuit diagram. The **cathode** $(-)$ is normally denoted by a band around one end of the diode (Figure 6.5a).

The semiconductor material is generally silicon or germanium, contained in a glass,

(a)

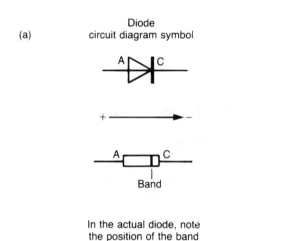

In the actual diode, note the position of the band

(c)

Zener diode

(d)

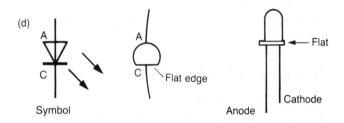

Light Emitting Diode (LED)

(b)

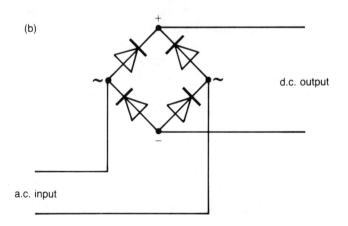

Four diodes wired as a bridge rectifier

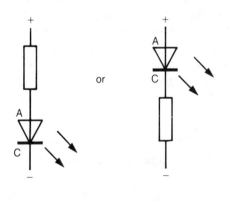

LED and series resistor

Figure 6.5 Diodes

plastic or metal case. Modern silicon diodes are fairly tough, and may be soldered without any special precautions. Avoid excessive heat if possible – particularly when desoldering if you are unfortunate enough to have to do so.

Applications

Diodes may be used to convert alternating current (a.c.) to direct current (d.c.); to 'steer' current in logic circuits; to protect equipment against accidentally connecting the supply the wrong way round, and in many other areas.

Types

Diodes are available in such a wide range of types that they are given code numbers. For example the 1N4001 silicon diode is rated at 1 A, 50 V. This means that it will withstand a *reverse* voltage of up to 50 V, or conduct a forward current of up to 1 A. It costs just a few pence and is an ideal general purpose diode.

Buying guide

When ordering, quote the *type number* required.

Bridge rectifiers

As mentioned before, diodes are often used in power supplies to convert a.c. into d.c. To achieve a 'full wave' conversion (described in Chapter 3, 'Variable voltage regulator'), four diodes are often used, connected in a 'bridge circuit' (Figure 6.5b). A bridge rectifier is simply four diodes connected in this way, but enclosed in a complete package with only four connecting leads. It is quite popular, as time is saved in assembly; however, a bridge rectifier is often more expensive than buying four separate diodes.

Buying guide

When ordering, either quote the type number, or the *voltage* and *current* required.

Zener diodes

When a voltage is connected in reverse to a zener diode, the diode does not conduct until a certain value is reached. The voltage across the zener diode is then maintained at a fairly steady level even if the current rises. This voltage can be set when the diode is manufactured, and the zener is therefore used as a voltage reference. For example, a zener diode may be used to provide a constant 9 V supply from a 12 V source. The beginner is not advised to use this simple arrangement in practice, as great care must be taken regarding the power required.

Buying guide

When ordering, quote the *type number* and *voltage* required.

Light emitting diodes (LED)

The light emitting diode (LED) is a semiconductor device which looks like a tiny light bulb. It uses less power and is virtually everlasting. Electricity must be supplied in the correct direction, and *never connect a LED directly to any supply*. The reason is that like any diode, very little forward resistance is offered to electricity, and a large current will therefore flow. LEDs must always be used with a resistor connected in series as shown in Figure 6.5d. LEDs are available in various colours, including red (the most common), green, yellow and orange. Red is the least expensive, and provides the most light for the least current. In fact, a current of only 10 mA will make a red LED glow quite brightly. The other colours may require more current – achieved by using a lower value series resistor as shown in the table below.

The value of the resistor is calculated according to the voltage being used. This is described fully later, but the following is a convenient guide for popular voltages with 10 to 20 mA LEDs.

Voltage (in volts)	Resistor required	
	Red LED	Other colours
12	1 kΩ	560 Ω
9	680 Ω (1k will do)	330 Ω
6	470 Ω	220 Ω
4.5 to 5	270 Ω	150 Ω
3	150 Ω	56 Ω

These values of resistors will provide red LEDs with about 10 mA, and the other colours with about 20 mA. The actual resistor used need not correspond exactly to that shown above; for example, it is quite in order to use a resistor from 500 Ω to 1000 Ω with a red (10 mA) LED on a 9 V supply.

Calculating LED series resistors
When calculating the value required, we need to know two figures concerning the LED. (Most good catalogues provide the required information.) These figures are:
1 The current required by the LED.
2 The forward voltage drop produced by the LED.

Many red LEDs require a current of about 10 mA, while the other colours may require about 20 mA. A new range of LEDs is available with an average recommended current of 2 mA (maximum current 7 mA).

The forward voltage drop of a typical LED is about 2 V. In other words there will always be a potential difference of 2 V across such an LED. Thus, to work at all, the voltage used in the circuit must be greater than 2 V.

The formula used to calculate the value of the series resistor must include the total voltage across the LED and resistor combined (total voltage), the forward voltage drop across the LED (V_{drop}) and the current required (current).

$$\text{series resistor} = \frac{\text{total voltage} - V_{drop}}{\text{current}}$$

Note that the voltage is in volts, the current in amps and the series resistor in ohms. A useful short-cut is to write the current in milliamps (mA), in which case the series resistor value will be in kilo-ohms (kΩ).

Example 1
We wish to use a red LED on a 6 V supply. The current required is 10 mA and the forward voltage drop is 2 V.

$$\text{series resistor (in k}\Omega) = \frac{6 - 2}{10}$$

$$= \frac{4}{10}$$

$$= 0.4 \text{ k}\Omega = 400 \text{ }\Omega$$

Example 2
We wish to use a low current LED on 6 V. The LED requires a current of 2 mA and has a forward voltage drop of 1.8 V.

$$\text{series resistor (in k}\Omega) = \frac{6 - 1.8}{2}$$

$$= \frac{4.2}{2}$$

$$= 2.1 \text{ k}\Omega = 2100 \text{ }\Omega$$

When buying a suitable resistor, the nearest standard value should be obtained. A resistor of any power rating and tolerance may be used, since the current flowing is small and the exact value is unimportant. In other words buy the smallest, cheapest resistor.

LEDs in series
LEDs may be wired in series, provided an equal current is required by each and the total voltage available is greater than the voltage drops of the LEDs added together. This total V_{drop} must be used in the formula. The current will be as for one LED. They should be wired cathode–anode, cathode–anode, etc.

LEDs are sold in all shapes and sizes; round LEDs have diameters of 3 mm or 5 mm. Rectangular and triangular types are available, as are special low-power types and high intensity types. Other types include LED arrays plus a wide range of seven segment displays which, by lighting the appropriate segments, produce illuminated numbers.

Buying guide

Buy LEDs from a reputable supplier. Beware of special offers as the quality varies a great deal.

When ordering, quote the *colour, shape,* and *size* required.

Transistors, Thyristors and Triacs

A transistor is a semiconductor device which generally has three leads. It normally consists of a chip of silicon or germanium inside a plastic or metal case. A transistor can behave like a control valve, where a

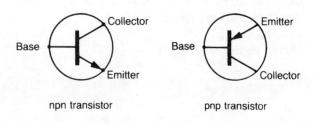

npn transistor   pnp transistor

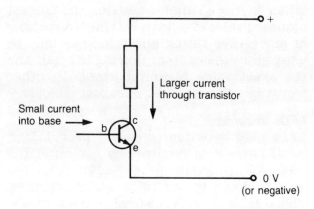

Small current into base →

Larger current through transistor

0 V (or negative)

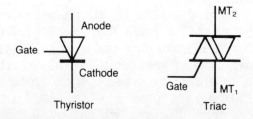

Thyristor   Triac

Figure 6.6 Transistors

small input current controls a larger output current. It can therefore amplify (increase the size of) a signal. In many circuits a transistor is used as a switch, where a small input current switches on its output. (See Figure 6.6.)

When designing circuits it is important to remember that no current will flow into the base of a silicon transistor, unless the voltage is a little over half a volt (0.6 V for many small transistors).

Types

Transistors are divided into two main types: npn and pnp. These must never be confused, as one type may burn out if fitted in place of the other. Code numbers are used to identify transistors. At present, npn transistors tend to be more popular, and the following are examples of some low-power npn types:

BC184L, BC183L, BC182L, BC107, BC108, BC109, ZTX300, 2N3705

In general, the type number specified in a circuit should be adhered to. However, some constructors like to use substitutes — particularly if a similar type happens to be in the spares box.

Connections

The three leads are called the base, collector and emitter. In an npn transistor, a small flow of current into the base connection causes a much larger current to flow from the collector to emitter. This ratio of output current to input current is known as the **gain**.

Transistor variations

All the npn transistors required in this book are type BC184L. This transistor offers a high gain at a very low price, and is packaged in a plastic case with 'in line' leads. Beware of purchasing BC184 (without the 'L') transistors — the leads are in a different order (see Chapter 1), even though the transistor is similar in other respects.

Another popular range of transistors is types BC107, BC108, BC109. These often end with a letter A, B or C. This last letter — if present — indicates the gain. Letter 'A' indicates lowest gain and letter 'C' the highest. It is acceptable to use a transistor with a *higher* gain than indicated in a circuit, but poor results may be obtained by using a lower gain transistor. Some suppliers only sell high-gain 'C' transistors, as they are hardly more expensive than lower gain types.

The BC184L transistors specified in this book may be replaced by BC108C transistors if desired. *But*, do note carefully the positions of the leads: the base lead of a BC184L transistor is on the outside, whereas the base lead of a BC108C transistor is between the other two leads as shown in the diagrams in Chapter 1. You may well find that any of the low-power transistors listed above will work in place of BC184L types, but this cannot be guaranteed.

Using transistors

Transistors used to be very delicate, and could only be soldered using a 'heat sink' (a piece of metal clipped to the lead being soldered, to conduct away the heat). Modern silicon transistors are more hardy, and no precautions need be taken when soldering. If you have to de-solder a transistor, do so as quickly as possible, using a heat sink if available. Transistor holders are available, allowing a transistor to be plugged in without soldering. This may sound a good idea, but a holder may well be more expensive than a low-power transistor!

Thyristors and triacs

A thyristor, sometimes called a silicon controlled rectifier (SCR), is rather like a transistor in that it has three connections, and current into the 'gate' (like the 'base') switches it on. Unlike a transistor, the thyristor, once switched on, will stay on, even if no current continues to flow into the gate. It only switches off when the supply is removed. This 'holding on' or 'latching' effect can be very useful, as illustrated in Chapter 2.

Thyristors are useful in a.c. power control. The more expensive types can handle high voltages (including mains – 240 V a.c.), and quite high currents. The fact that thyristors only conduct in one direction can be a slight disadvantage, bearing in mind that a.c. flows in both directions.

Triacs (also known as bi-directional silicon controlled rectifiers) overcome this problem. A triac behaves like a double thyristor, which when turned on by means of a current into its gate conducts in either direction. Thus in an a.c. circuit it can switch on with very little power loss. Triacs have become very popular for use in mains a.c. circuits, including 'dimmer switches', motor speed controllers etc.

Buying guide

Transistors, thyristors and triacs all have code numbers. If in doubt, buy exactly the code specified. With some experience, you may make substitutes. Good quality catalogues often include 'data pages' which list the main factors associated with a particular type of transistor etc. Such data is valuable to experienced constructors in selecting components for newly designed circuits, or for checking whether another type may be substituted.

Relays

Relays are very useful as they allow one electronic circuit to control another circuit with no electrical link between the two. For example, a project may be required to control a 240 V mains circuit. The use of a relay will allow the mains circuits to be switched on or off, without any fear of the mains finding its way into the delicate electronic control circuit. This assumes that the relay is wired correctly!

Basically, a relay is an electromagnetic switch. It consists of a coil wound around a soft iron core, and a movable 'armature' also made of soft iron. When electricity is passed through the coil, the soft iron core becomes magnetised and attracts the armature. The armature in turn closes (turns on) a switch contact. Such a switch contact is called a normally open (n/o) (or 'make') contact, as it is open (off) when the relay is not energised. Many relays also have 'normally closed' (n/c) (or 'break') contacts. Such

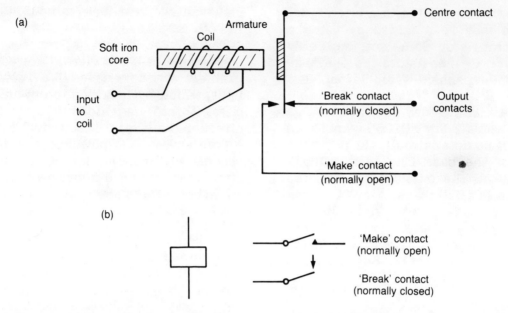

(a)

Centre contact

Armature

Coil

Soft iron core

Input to coil

'Break' contact
(normally closed)

Output contacts

'Make' contact
(normally open)

(b)

'Make' contact
(normally open)

'Break' contact
(normally closed)

Figure 6.7 (a) Relay with a changeover contact; (b) relay circuit diagram symbol

contacts are normally closed (on) when the relay is not energised, but open (off) when current flows into the relay coil. The relay illustrated in Figure 6.7 has a 'changeover' contact which is a combined 'make-and-break' contact.

A word of caution: when relay coils switch off, the sudden loss of magnetism in the core induces (generates) a high voltage across the coil. This voltage (known as 'back e.m.f.') may be sufficient to burn out a transistor. The problem is easily cured by the addition of a diode which *must* be connected the correct way round as shown in Figure 6.8. This diode 'shorts out' the unwanted voltage produced by the relay. Note that if the diode is connected the wrong way round, a large current will flow directly to the transistor and may destroy it.

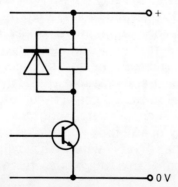

Figure 6.8 The diode is required to protect the transistor from back e.m.f. produced by the relay coil.

Many types of diodes are suitable for this application, such as types 1N4001 or 1N4148. A similar effect is produced by electric motors, bells and buzzers with make-and-break contacts. If any of these devices are connected *directly* to a transistor, a protecting diode must be used.

Selecting a relay

A very wide range of relays is available. The most important points to note are the coil voltage, coil resistance, and voltage and current rating of the relay contacts. The size and shape of the relay may also be important if space is limited. Some relays are designed to plug directly into stripboard or printed circuit boards. This is not very desirable if mains voltages are to be controlled by the relay – unless very great care is taken.

If the relay is to be used with a BC184L or similar transistor, a 12 V type should have a coil resistance of 150 Ω or more. A 6 V type should have a coil resistance of 100 Ω or more. The coil voltage should correspond to the voltage used in the circuit though many 12 V relays work satisfactorily on 9 V and many 6 V relays work on 4.5 V or 5 V. A good quality components catalogue will state the exact voltage range for each relay. If a relay coil is connected to a transistor, note that the voltage across the relay coil will be about 0.5 V less than the supply.

Ensure that the relay contacts have a higher voltage rating than the voltage you wish to control. The same applies to their current rating.

Many relays have more than one set of contacts, and this can be important in some circuits. Virtually all relays have 'normally open' (n/o) contacts; many have 'normally closed' (n/c) contacts as well, and some have 'changeover' contacts as illustrated in Figure 6.7.

Buying guide

Check the coil voltage and coil resistance. Ensure that the contacts have a higher voltage and current rating than required. Check that the number and type of contacts included is as required.

Integrated Circuits

An integrated circuit (IC) is a complete electronic circuit formed in a small chip of silicon or other semiconductor material. Once a design is perfected, copies can be produced very cheaply. Thus the price of a complete integrated circuit is sometimes little more than that of a single transistor. Many types of electronic components may be present in the 'chip': transistors, diodes, resistors and small capacitors – though these are more difficult to incorporate.

The chip of silicon may measure only 1.5 mm square, and 0.2 mm thick. It must therefore be 'packaged' before it leaves the factory. Various types of packages are employed, but two are particularly common, namely the TO-5 transistor package (looking like a transistor with several more leads), and the plastic dual-in-line type.

The dual-in-line (DIL) package is popular and this is the type used in this book. Looking like a crude mechanical caterpillar, it consists of a plastic case housing the silicon chip, with two sets of pin connections down each side. The number of pins varies with the size and complexity of the integrated circuit, and may range from about 6 pins to 40 pins. When fitting an IC in a circuit, note the pin numbering system used. See Chapter 1 for details.

Integrated circuits offer many advantages over the use of discrete (individual component) circuits. They take up less space, are less expensive and more reliable. An integrated circuit normally requires at least some other components, and the use of ICs in circuit design has increased the scope of the amateur circuit builder enormously. Projects can now be constructed by an amateur which a few years ago would have been far too complicated.

Linear integrated circuits

Linear ICs are usually designed to operate with signals of continuously varying voltages. Sometimes they amplify a signal. A good example of this type of IC is the operational amplifier type 741, as used in Chapter 3. Another example is the type LM380. This is specially designed for audio (sound) amplification, and forms the basis of the amplifier also described in Chapter 3.

This type of circuit can handle 'analogue' information. That is, a signal which can be of any voltage between its highest and lowest levels.

Digital integrated circuits

This type of IC is designed to handle digital information. Digital ICs normally operate with signals of only two voltage levels. The level may be 'high' (nearly equal to the supply voltage) or 'low' (nearly equal to zero volts). The logic circuits described in Chapter 4 employ this type of IC.

Digital circuits may be designed to count and process numbers, and can therefore form the basis of computers and related equipment. Since their signals are of two distinct voltage levels there is little risk of confusion between a 'low' or a 'high'.

Logic Integrated Circuits

Logic circuits sound mysterious and complicated to the newcomer. In fact they are probably more straightforward than most linear circuits. Logic circuits are normally digital. In other words, they work with on's and off's; the 'on' state is normally represented by a '1' and 'off' is represented by '0'. This clear difference makes logic circuits very reliable and fairly immune to interference from other sources.

Logic circuits may be built using relays or individual transistors and associated components. In practice it is more convenient to use integrated circuits (ICs), which are less expensive, involve less wiring and are more reliable.

Several ranges of general purpose logic ICs are in common use, and these are briefly outlined as follows.

Standard 74 (TTL) series
TTL stands for **transistor transistor logic**, and this series of ICs is designed for operation on exactly 5 V. The series is now rather dated.

74LS (TTL) series
This family has largely replaced the standard 74 series and performs the same tasks at increased speed, using much less current. Again, they are designed for operation on a voltage range from 4.75 V to 5.25 V. In practice they will probably work with a new 4.5 V battery, but ideally they should be powered using a 5 V regulator such as the one described in Chapter 3. They are easy to handle and reliable in operation. In some respects their electrical characteristics are less than ideal and impose restrictions on circuit designs.

74ALS (TTL) series
This is an even more efficient series than the 74LS range. They are directly compatible with the 74LS range and operate twice as quickly using half the power. They may be more expensive however.

Complementary metal-oxide semiconductors (CMOS)
CMOS technology can form the basis of linear ICs or digital ICs. The original CMOS logic series is known as the CMOS 4000 family.

CMOS 4000 logic ICs have certain advantages over TTL types. They use very little power, resulting in batteries lasting many months or years. They will work on a voltage range of about 3 to 15 V, and have a very high input resistance. This means that almost no current is required at the input of a CMOS IC. Circuit designers frequently exploit this fact, touch-sensitive switches being one of many applications.

The very high input resistance has one disadvantage, however. When you touch a wire of a normal component, any static charge in your body quickly 'earths' through the component, reducing the voltage to zero. The current is too small to cause any damage, even though a static voltage may be over 1000 V (especially if you have just walked across a nylon carpet!). If you touch the input of a CMOS IC, its resistance is so high that almost no current flows; the voltage in your body therefore remains high, and may destroy the IC.

Thus some care is necessary when handling CMOS ICs. They are supplied in special conductive foam, conductive plastic or foil, which offers complete protection until removed. Once installed in a circuit they are unlikely to be damaged, as the other components will 'earth' the static charges. The danger period is when they are transferred from their protective packing to the circuit. If this can be done without touching the pins, all will be well. If the pins are likely to be touched, a wise precaution is to place your hand on an 'earthed' metal surface for a second or so. A cold water tap may serve this purpose, or the metal frame of an appliance plugged into the mains supply, but not necessarily switched on. Once 'earthed' you should not pose a threat to a CMOS IC, for a short time at least.

It is essential to use an IC holder when using CMOS ICs in a stripboard circuit, as it would be difficult to solder their pins directly without damage. In practice it is wise to use holders for all ICs whether or not they are CMOS types.

The slight risk of damage to a CMOS IC should not deter the constructor. The advantages of using this type of circuit are enormous by comparison.

High speed CMOS 74HC and 74HCT

These ranges of ICs combine the advantages of CMOS technology with TTL ICs. Standard TTL circuits are much faster than standard CMOS circuits. While this difference in operating speed is of no importance to the circuits in this book, operating speed is important in some equipment, such as computers. This latest range of ICs combines the low power requirements of CMOS ICs with the high speed of TTL ICs.

The 74HC series will operate on voltages ranging from 2 to 6 V, while the 74HCT series is designed for 5 V only operation, with inputs and outputs totally compatible with the original TTL ranges. The very low current required by the inputs of the CMOS 4000 range applies to these ranges also. The excellent electrical characteristics make the 74HC (and 74HCT) series very useful to circuit designers.

There is a possibility that these new ranges will eventually supersede the standard TTL, 74LS TTL, 74ALS TTL and CMOS 4000 series.

Selecting your IC

The two types of ICs included in Chapter 4 are taken from the 74HC (CMOS) and the 74LS (TTL) ranges. The 74HC (CMOS) type is superior in almost every respect, especially if powered with a battery. Its one disadvantage is that it can be damaged by static electricity and requires careful handling. The 74LS (TTL) IC may be freely handled and can be used instead of the CMOS IC in many of the circuits in Chapter 4 if preferred. Note that each IC has its own code number. The type used mainly in Chapter 4 is '02'. Thus the two versions of this IC are:

74HC02 (CMOS) and 74LS02 (TTL)

When ordering, it is not necessary to state 'CMOS' or 'TTL', as this is apparent from the code.

Understanding how logic integrated circuits are used

The following information applies equally to all the types of logic ICs listed above.

Electrical states
There are two electrical states as outlined earlier. These are called by various names as follows:

'HIGH' (nearly equal to the positive supply voltage)
        Sometimes called 'hi' or logic 1
'LOW'   (nearly equal to zero volts)
        Sometimes called 'lo' or logic 0

Gates (See Figure 6.9)
A single logic gate consists of a complete circuit comprising transistors and other components inside the IC, and designed to produce a clear output which may be either 'high' or 'low'. The following gates are in common use in circuits.

Buffer gate A single buffer produces a 'low' output when its input is 'low' and a 'high' output when its input is 'high'.

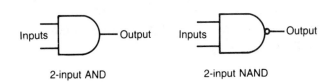

Figure 6.9 Logic gates

Inverter (sometimes called a NOT) gate This produces a 'high' output when its input is 'low' and a 'low' output when its input is 'high'.

2-input OR gate If both inputs are 'low' the output is 'low'. If one input, OR the other (or both) are 'high' then the output is 'high'.

2-input NOR gate If both inputs are 'low' the output is 'high'. If one OR the other (or both) inputs are 'high' then the output goes 'low'. (It is like an OR gate joined to a NOT gate.)

2-input AND gate If both inputs are 'low' the output is 'low'. If only one input is 'high' the output remains 'low'. If one input AND the other go 'high', then the output goes 'high'. In other words, only if *both* inputs are 'high' will the output go 'high'.

2-input NAND gate When both inputs are 'low' the output is 'high'. If only one input is 'high' then the output remains 'high'. If both inputs go 'high' then the output goes 'low'. (It is like an AND gate joined to a NOT gate.)

For simplicity the descriptions above have included gates with only one or two inputs. Gates are also available with three or more inputs. The theory behind such gates is very similar. For example, a 3-input NAND gate will produce a 'high' output if either no inputs, or one input, or two inputs are 'high'. If all three inputs are 'high', the output will change to 'low'.

Truth tables
The examples described above are quite simple, yet appear complicated when expressed in normal English. Truth tables provide a more visual summary of the same details. The words 'high' and 'low' may be used, but it is quicker to express a truth table in 1's and 0's. Both methods are used in the examples below, which illustrate the use of truth tables and the logic gates described above.

Buffer gate:

input	output	input	output
low	low	0	0
high	high	1	1

Inverter gate (NOT):

input	output	input	output
low	high	0	1
high	low	1	0

OR gate (with 2 inputs):

input A	input B	output	input A	input B	output
low	low	low	0	0	0
high	low	high	1	0	1
low	high	high	0	1	1
high	high	high	1	1	1

NOR gate (with 2 inputs):

input A	input B	output	input A	input B	output
low	low	high	0	0	1
high	low	low	1	0	0
low	high	low	0	1	0
high	high	low	1	1	0

AND gate (with 2 inputs):

input A	input B	output	input A	input B	output
low	low	low	0	0	0
high	low	low	1	0	0
low	high	low	0	1	0
high	high	high	1	1	1

NAND gate (with 2 inputs):

input A	input B	output	input A	input B	output
low	low	high	0	0	1
high	low	high	1	0	1
low	high	high	0	1	1
high	high	low	1	1	0

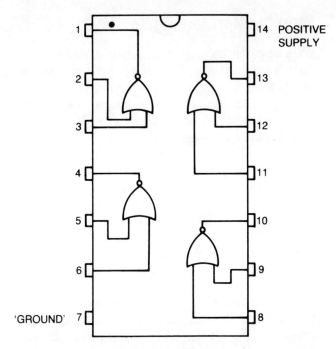

Figure 6.10 Pin connections for the quadruple 2-input NOR gate IC (type 02): examples are 74HC02 and 74LS02

Several gates are normally housed in one IC 'package'. For example six buffer or six inverter gates are housed in one 14 pin IC, whereas the other 2-input gates described are housed in groups of four. An IC used frequently in Chapter 4 is a 'Quadruple 2-input NOR gate', otherwise known as type '02'. The pin arrangement is shown in Figure 6.10.

More complex logic

The gates described may be used for a wide variety of mathematical tasks. They can be made to count, switch and sort information, produce waves and operate as timers. Any good electronics catalogue will list a range of integrated circuits which perform the functions described.

Fault Finding

If your circuit fails to work, don't despair — you are in good company! Electronic equipment manufacturers employ technicians whose sole purpose is to repair faults in brand new equipment. When you consider that the slightest bridge of solder, a hairline crack, a dry joint, a lead in the wrong place, will all prevent a circuit working, it is surprising that a circuit ever works the first time.

Many beginners immediately suspect a faulty component. While this may be the case if you have used second-hand parts it is the least likely cause if you purchased new components.

Begin by making a visual check — but do not study your circuit for too long. Unless the fault is very obvious you may stare at the circuit for hours without spotting the mistake. These are the likely errors:

General faults

1 Leads or wires in the wrong place.
2 Components fitted the wrong way round — check especially the transistors, diodes, LEDs and electrolytic capacitors.
3 A missing wire link. Always count them carefully.
4 A forgotten component.

Additional stripboard faults

5 Adjacent stripboard tracks bridged with solder. Run a screwdriver blade between *every* pair of tracks — even if you cannot see a solder bridge.
6 Breaks in stripboard tracks either not made at all, or not made properly, or in the wrong places. Check them carefully and check that components are fitted the correct side of a break.
7 'Dry' solder joints. The solder should appear shiny and be in good contact with the stripboard track *and* component wire. Look again at the diagrams in Chapter 1 which illustrate this (page 6).
8 A crack in the stripboard track. Fortunately, this is not very common.
9 Fragments of copper shorting the tracks together. This happens when sawing the stripboard and when making breaks.

Step by step testing

This applies to any method of construction. As stated, you should not spend too long on the visual check as it is easy to miss even obvious mistakes. A more scientific approach should be used, where each part of the circuit is tested step by step.

Many of the circuits employ a transistor to switch on the output. Use a short piece of bare wire (even a clean small screwdriver blade will do) to short together the collector(c) and emitter(e) leads of the transistor. Make sure you short the correct leads — check with the diagram first. If the output now works, the fault lies either with the transistor itself or with the circuit feeding its base. If the output did not work, check the position of the transistor and the connections leading to the LED or whatever should have switched on. The same points apply to a thyristor, where you should short the anode and cathode together.

To test the output transistor, try connecting a resistor of about 1 kΩ from the positive supply to the transistor base (or thyristor gate). It should now turn on. If it does not, the transistor could be at fault, or the base connection could be shorting to the zero volts (or negative) line.

If the output from your circuit remains on all the time, there could be a short-circuit from collector to emitter. Disconnect (or cut) the resistor wire feeding the transistor base. If the output still remains on, the transistor is at fault, or wired incorrectly to the output.

Using a multimeter, voltmeter or voltmeter substitute

If you can measure voltage, there are a number of additional steps you can make to trace the fault. If you do not possess a voltmeter, you could build a crude substitute which will enable some tests to be made.

A voltmeter substitute may be made by joining a 1 kΩ resistor in series with a 10 mA LED. Ensure that you label or colour the wires accurately to indicate positive (red) and negative (black) as shown in

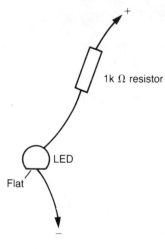

Figure 6.11

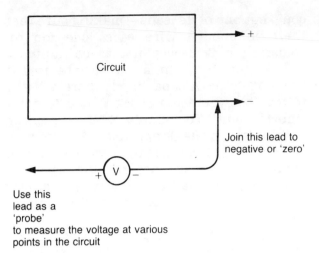

Figure 6.12

Figure 6.11. Test your 'substitute' with a supply of between 4 and 12 V to check that the LED does light. This device will not make measurements in a circuit, but will enable you to test that the supply is correctly connected throughout the circuit. If you have used 74HC ICs in Chapter 4, the 'substitute' may also be used to test the states of the *output* pins.

Locate the points in the circuit which should be connected to the positive and negative supplies and use a voltmeter (or substitute) to check them. If you obtain no reading, check the supply, check the connections from it and check for short-circuits. A short-circuit is a serious fault as it will quickly run down a battery. If you find that the battery voltage drops when you connect your circuit, either a short-circuit exists or the battery is worn out. If you are using either voltage regulator described in Chapter 3 a short-circuit will be apparent by the LED (on the regulator) failing to light when your circuit is connected. (This assumes that you are testing one of the circuits in this book — all of which use less than 100 mA current. If you have built a circuit which uses more current than the regulator can supply, the LED will also switch off.)

If the project employs integrated circuits, check the voltage across the positive and negative pins of the IC. This should be equal or nearly equal to the supply voltage.

Beyond this, you will need a proper voltmeter to check the voltages at points within

a circuit. Connect the negative lead to the negative or 'zero volts' point in the circuit as shown in Figure 6.12, and follow the 'Fault finding' and/or 'How it works' sections for the project described.

Testing components

As stated, new components are the least likely cause of trouble, but faulty components are sometimes supplied and components are sometimes damaged by the user or a fault in the circuit. In general, components (other than ICs) tend to either 'short-circuit' (acting like a wire link) or go 'open circuit' (behaving as though they were not fitted).

If you suspect a transistor, it may be tested using the 'soil moisture indicator' circuit in Chapter 2. Components are easy to remove from breadboard, but difficult to de-solder from stripboard. Providing you have left the leads long, and there is a space to the right or left of the transistor for it (or a substitute) to be re-connected, you could cut the leads near the stripboard. After testing (which is described under 'soil moisture indicator'), the transistor (or a substitute) may be re-soldered one or two holes to the right or left of its previous position — assuming that it connects to the same tracks as before. Ensure that you do not re-connect it the wrong side of a break.

If you suspect a particular resistor or capacitor and do not wish to remove it, you could cut one of its leads — making sure that there is enough wire each side for re-soldering if it proves not to be faulty. A multimeter set to 'Ohms' may now be used to test a resistor. A capacitor is more difficult to test, but you could check that it is not a 'short-circuit'. You should obtain a reading of 'infinity' on the Ohms range. A diode may be checked in a similar fashion. You should obtain a low resistance reading with the multimeter connected one way, and a very high resistance reading with the connections reversed.

Alternatively, having disconnected one side of a component, you could solder a new component across the same tracks as the old one and see if the circuit now works.

Above all, do not give up. Read the 'How it works' section and check the voltages at various points throughout the circuit. Many constructors who would otherwise have ignored the theory have been forced into an understanding of electronics by a failed project!

A Summary of Components

BATTERY A source of direct current

BUZZER Produces a sound when fed with electricity. Older buzzers had 'make-and-break' contacts, which can cause a high voltage (back e.m.f.) to be produced. Many modern buzzers are 'solid state' and do not produce a high voltage.

CAPACITOR Stores electrical energy (*see* page 121)

CHOKE A type of coil (often called an inductor)

CONDENSER As capacitor

DIAC A 'bi-directional diode thyristor' which acts like two zener diodes (*see* page 124) opposing one another. Often used for firing (switching on) triacs in mains dimmer circuits.

DIODE Allows electricity to flow in only one direction (*see* page 123)

EARPHONE Converts electrical signals into sound waves

FERRITE ROD AERIAL Converts radio waves into electrical signals

FUSE A deliberate weak link in a circuit, which is designed to 'blow' (melt) safely if too much current flows

INTEGRATED CIRCUIT (IC) A complete electronic circuit formed within a single chip of semiconductor material (*see* page 129)

LIGHT DEPENDENT RESISTOR (LDR) A light-sensitive resistor. As the light falling on it increases, its resistance falls

LIGHT EMITTING DIODE (LED) Converts electricity into light. Can be used to display numbers and letters (*see* page 124)

LIQUID CRYSTAL DISPLAY (LCD) Capable of displaying numbers and letters using very little electricity

LOUDSPEAKER Converts electrical signals into sound waves

MICROPHONE Converts sound waves into electrical signals

NEON Like a small lamp. Contains neon gas which glows when a high voltage is applied

OP-AMP Operational amplifiers are often integrated circuits which will amplify a.c. or d.c. signals (*see* page 54)

OPTO-ISOLATOR Comprises a LED and a light sensor. Light from the LED passes to the sensor, switching it on. An opto-isolator provides complete isolation between the control circuit and the circuit being switched

PHOTO-DIODE A diode which is electrically affected by light

PHOTO-TRANSISTOR A transistor which is electrically affected by light

POTENTIOMETER Often called a 'pot' or rheostat (*see* page 120)

PRESET A type of potentiometer (*see* page 120)

RECTIFIER A device or circuit which converts a.c. to d.c.

REED SWITCH A pair of magnetic switch contacts housed in a small glass container. When a magnet is brought near it, the contacts close (switch on). (Changeover reed switches are also available.)

RELAY An electrically operated switch (*see* page 127)

RESISTOR Reduces the flow of electricity (*see* page 118)

RHEOSTAT *See* POTENTIOMETER

SILICON CONTROLLED RECTIFIER (SCR) *See* THYRISTOR

SOLAR CELL (or PANEL) Converts light into electricity

SOLENOID A coil which can attract (by means of magnetism) a movable piece of soft iron towards its centre

SPEAKER *See* LOUDSPEAKER

THERMAL BREAKER Switches off automatically at a pre-determined temperature

THERMISTOR Rather like a resistor whose resistance is deliberately designed to change with temperature

THYRISTOR Works like a transistor except that, once switched on, it continues to conduct until the supply current is removed. Often used in a.c. mains circuits for light dimmer control (*see* page 126)

TRANSFORMER Often used to change voltages (and currents), or to isolate one supply from another. Works only on a.c.

TRANSISTOR *See* page 126

TRIAC Sometimes referred to as a bi-directional silicon controlled rectifier. Used extensively in mains dimmer controls and similar applications, where a small current input will control a larger alternating current (*see* page 126)

VARIABLE RESISTOR *See* POTENTIO-
METER

VARICAP DIODE   A diode which behaves like a variable capacitor

ZENER DIODE   *See* page 124